April Shenandoah

#246 of 2500 Special First Edition

Presented

To _President Clinton_

By _April Shenandoah_

Date _February 4, 1999_

A Prophecy
from the 1600's, foretelling the future.

After the year 1900, toward the middle of the 20th century, the people of that time will become unrecognizable. When the time for the advent of the Antichrist approaches, people's minds will grow cloudy from carnal passions, and dishonor and lawlessness will grow stronger. Then they will become unrecognizable. People's appearances will change, and it will be impossible to distinguish men from women due to their shamelessness in dress and style of hair. These people will be cruel and will be like wild animals because of the temptation of the Antichrist. There will be no respect for parents and elders; love will disappear.

Christian pastors, bishops and priests will become vain men, completely failing to distinguish the right hand way from the left. At that time the morals and traditions of Christians and of the Church will change. People will abandon modesty, and dissipation will reign. Falsehood and greed will attain great proportions, and woe to those who pile up treasures. Lust end adultery, homosexuality, secret deeds, and murder will rule in society. At that future time, due to the power of such great crimes and licentiousness, people will be deprived of the grace of the Holy Spirit, which they receive in the Holy Baptism, and equally of remorse.

The churches of God will be deprived of God-fearing and pious pastors, and woe to the Christians remaining in the world at that time; they will completely lose their faith because they will lack the opportunity of seeing the light of knowledge from anyone at all. Then they will separate themselves out of the world in holy refuge in search of enlightening of their spiritual sufferings, but everywhere they will meet obstacles and constraints. And all this will result from the act that the Antichrist wants to be Lord over everything and become the ruler of the whole universe, and he will produce miracles and fantastic signs. He will also give depraved wisdom to an unhappy man so that he will discover a way by which one man can carry on a conversation with another from one end of the earth to the other.

At that time men will also fly through the air like birds and descend to the bottom of the sea like fishes. And when they have achieved all this, these unhappy people will spend their lives in comfort without knowing, poor souls, that it is the deceit of the Antichrist, and the ungodly one! He will so complete science with vanity that it will go off the right path and lead people to lose faith in the existence of God in three hypostases.

Then the All-Good God will see the downfall of the human race and will shorten the days for the sake of those few who are being saved, because the enemy wants to lead even the chosen into temptation, if that is possible. Then the sword of chastisement will suddenly appear and kill the perverder and his servants.

Saint Nilos,
A Hermit and Myrr-streaming of Mt. Athos, Greece
--Died Nov. 12, 1651--

So...Help Me God!

So...Help Me God!

AN INSPIRED LETTER TO
PRESIDENT WILLIAM JEFFERSON CLINTON

April Shenandoah

Eden Street Productions
Beverly Hills, California

The words "So help me God" were first inserted into the Oath of Office for the Presidency of the United States by General George Washington at his first presidential inauguration. Since that time every President has repeated "So help me God", regardless of their faith, thereby recognizing that their high office is a sacred one.

> *"The propitious smiles of Heaven can never be expected on a nation that disregards the eternal rules of order and right which Heaven itself has ordained."*
>
> George Washington, 1789, Inaugural Address

First Edition
10 9 8 7 6 5 4 3 2

Book design: Rudy Milanovich

A Prophecy of Saint Nilos: Contributed by Tony Nassif

Presentation graphic reprinted from King James, Illustrated Bible, World Publishers, Copyright 1954.

Scripture quotations are from the Holy Bible: King James Version

Library of Congress Cataloging-in-Publication Data
98-092293

ISBN 0-9666517-0-7

Eden Street Productions
PO Box 854
Beverly Hills, CA 90213

Printed in the United States of America

Table of Contents

Dedication

This book is dedicated to the courageous forefathers who went before us and to all the fathers and the fatherless of America. To the fathers who fought for freedom and died for freedom, leaving their Sons and Daughters fatherless. To the fathers who returned from wars to find that their families had abandoned them. To the many fatherless men and women who may have never known their natural father and are still longing to fill the void. And especially to our Heavenly Father, who is the Father of us all and the only One who can and will fill that void.

Acknowledgments

Special Thanks To...

Charles E. Brookhart
Victor Chartrand
Velma Hagar
Michael Heyden
Rose Heyden
Eric Holzaphfel
Angelica Holzaphfel
Trish Lenihan
Tom Lester
Marvin J. Lovelien
Robert MacDonald
Courtney MacDonald
Gerald Nordskog
Tim Perior
Larry Poland
Herb Rogers
Evelyn Underwood
Bob Yerkes

and

Rudy Milanovich

Rudy, for your endless hours of work on this project and for your expertise on every level, Thank you! Your patience and demeanor was a joy to behold, especially when you didn't flinch while making the many changes. I honestly do not know how I would have completed this book without you. Let's do another one, so we can continue our stimulating conversations on solving the worlds problems.

Preface

President Clinton, during your speech at the National Prayer Breakfast in Washington D. C. in 1993, I was deeply inspired, little did I know to what extent. Your remarks resounded in my mind, (paraphrasing) "When I was sworn in I wanted to sound like a statesman and repeat with confidence, SO HELP ME GOD, however, in my mind I was hearing, "SO.......HELP ME GOD!" I remember thinking,what a great title for a book.

After returning to California, while having lunch with my pastor friend, Eric Holzaphfel, I told him I was going to write a book, but I didn't know what kind of book it was to be. He encouraged me and told me, "You'll know when the time comes". A year and a half went by and those words SO.......HELP ME GOD consistantly rang in my ear.

Finally I said, "Okay God, if you want me to write a book you open the doors and show me what to do and where to go, you help me bring it about." Before I had time to think about it, I was on an adventure in the name of Bill Clinton.

My time spent in Arkansas, with some of your friends and relatives, was most enjoyable. Everything I did on this research trip, concerning you, seemed as if it was an assignment straight from heaven. I will always remember the wonderful people of Arkansas, who treated me royally.

Though this letter/book is addressed to you, President William Jefferson Clinton, the content is for all of us to digest. It comes from the heart. Included are some articles that you might think a bit strong, however, the contents echo the feelings and thoughts of most of the Judeo-Christian population. If my own words seem harsh at times, I do not mean them to be. I wanted to freely express myself without dancing around the issues.

When all is said and done...

To God Be the Glory,

April Shenandoah

To The Friends of Arkansas...

You were very brave to be a part of this special tribute without knowing the contents of this letter. The opinions set forth are strictly my own. I appreciate and thank all of you who contributed your support, your time, your quotes and articles, making this a completed "treasure book".

Thank you for reading this labor of love.

August 19, 1998

President Bill Clinton
The White House
1600 Pennsylvania Ave.
Washington D. C. 20500-2000

Dear President Clinton,

The day you were elected President of these United States of America, I paced the floor and wept in disbelief. The haunting thought, "we have lost the country" pounded in my head. Very soon I realized I was not the only person having a migraine over the election. (As you read on, you will learn how my thoughts soon took a different turn.)

Let me back up. Here you came this charming good looking man, it seemed as if out of nowhere, even Republicans sat up and took notice. To my surprise, I was mesmerized by your speech at the Democratic convention. I wanted to hear what you had to say and believe in you. However, as the months went by and I listened to your ideas for "CHANGE" it was soon evident that the policies you favored were not for the good of the country. They may be good for political gain and the NEW WORLD ORDER, but not for flag-waving Americans like myself.

The first time I heard President Bush say the words "NEW WORLD ORDER" it was as if a knife went thru my heart. What I had learned as a child was coming to pass. The end times the Bible speaks of, were here!

No matter how anyone tries to explain it, "NEW WORLD ORDER" means an all-powerful, one-world government controlled by the United Nations.

This *Global Oneness* may sound good to those who reject Biblical truth and have forgotten the lessons of history. Global peace may sound good to those who want security and have never known political oppression. Global controls may sound good to those who fear terrorism more than totalitarianism. President Clinton, are you prepared to live with the fact that you are helping to sacrifice America's freedom, to fulfill a utopian dream that is headed for a nightmare of one-world dictatorship?

Over 200 years ago, Patrick Henry thundered at others who wanted peace at any price. "Forbid it, Almighty God," he roared.

The Constitution

After recognizing God from Whom we get our rights, the founding fathers hammered out a Constitution to limit government and to allow the people to govern themselves. There is no other nation with as praiseworthy a beginning as ours.

Mr. President, I have included the Constitution and the Declaration of Independence in the back of this book for your personal reference and for those who may never have laid eyes on them. I encourage everyone who is not familiar with these precious documents to read first hand what our forefathers set before us. We say the Constitution is important to us while at the same time we are so ignorant of it. When surveyed by the National Constitution Center, 25% could not name a single one of the four rights guaranteed by the First Amendment (freedom of speech, religion, press, and assembly), and only 6% could name all four.

We the People

"Our Constitution was made only for moral and religious people. It is inadequate to the government of any other."
—John Adams

January, 1993 was a very busy month filled with mixed emotions. January 8th the Elvis stamp was issued, two days later I attended Shepherd of the Hills Church in Chatsworth, Ca. and heard Elvis's stepbrother, Rick Stanley, preach and share his powerful testimony. January 11th, a precious lady friend, Valerie Caplin, went to be with the Lord. Valerie was one of several special ladies belonging to Bonnie Green's Covenant Prayer Group that I have been privileged to be a part of for many years. Then we have January 20th, Inauguration Day, certainly a happy day for you and yours, though a sad day for many others. Jan Adams, another dear friend from the same prayer group, was attending her husbands funeral. While she was mourning her loss, others were mourning the loss of America. Forgive me, I know that sounds cruel. It must have been the most important day of your life. On the 24th, I enjoyed my Son Robert's birthday dinner with him in Las Vegas. Well enough of January, follow me into February you may begin to like me a little.

National Prayer Breakfast

February 2nd, I was on a plane headed for Washington, D.C. to attend the National Prayer Breakfast. The morning of the breakfast was very special, a room full of dignitaries from all over the world with Billy Graham as the keynote speaker. Remember, just three months ago, I was devastated at the outcome of the election, now I find myself sitting just a holler away from you. My eyes were glued to your every move and expression. I don't know what I was looking for but what happened was nothing short of a miracle.

In what seemed like an instant, my heart was filled with supernatural, unconditional love for you. The negative thoughts were gone! It was nothing you said, or nothing you did, it was not you who changed my thinking. It became very clear that I was to leave the judging to God, my job was, and is, to pray for you and to tell others to do the same. This was definitely divine intervention, after all, it was a prayer breakfast. This does not mean that I agree with your decisions, it simply means I know how precious your soul is, and that there is a far greater plan for your life than being President.

Donna Rice's Wedding Shower

Thinking that Washington, D.C. was the perfect place to start my research for this book, I phoned Mary Doremus, a dear lady whom I had met at the Prayer Breakfast. She said that if I was ever in Washington to come and stay with her and her husband, Ted. It was perfect timing, as she was giving Donna Rice a wedding shower. Mary's house was Donna's retreat when she went into seclusion after the Gary Hart scandal.

This is my opportunity to let you all know that Donna is a precious woman of God. She turned her trials into triumphs by giving her life over to the Lord. She would visit Bonnie's prayer group on Thursday afternoon when she was in California. It was then I had the privilege of getting to know her. It may also surprise you to know that her IQ is off the charts.

The day I arrived, Mary was surrounded by many party guests, everyone was congratulating the bride to be. While talking with Donna, she told me she was going to be married at the Monmouth Plantation in Natchez, Mississippi. I was thrilled, Monmouth had been on my list of places to go for sometime. Lani Riches (also a member of Bonnie's prayer group) and her husband Ron are the proprietors of Monmouth.

Monmouth Plantation

In a couple of weeks, we were all headed to Mississippi to stay at the plantation for what was a spectacular, southern wedding. Mary Doremus and Lani Riches met for the first time. Those of us who know them suspected they would be friends at first sight, and they were! They are the essence of sweetness and light, full of love and long on hugs and kisses. If you invited them to Capital Hill on a regular basis, they would soon have the Democrats and Republicans seeing eye to eye.

When Lani discovered I was writing a book with you in mind, she mentioned that you had been a guest at Monmouth while you were governor. She suggested that I might want to interview

Marguerite Guercio, the overseer, who was in charge during your stay. She was a joy to talk with. Who ever coined the phrase "southern hospitality" must have had Marquerite in mind, I was blessed knowing her for those brief moments.

As she was reminiscing about your visit, she dubbed you and Hilliary "couple of the year". "They hugged and touched each other all the time and were not trying to impress anyone", she said. She told me she knew you were going to be President, and said, "I never met anyone with such charisma and charm and he is also brilliant".

I wish you could have heard Marguerite's enthusiasm as she spoke of you. It was as if she had never in her life met anyone quite like you. Her face lit up as she repeated over and over "he is the warmest, kindest, full of life, full of goodness, so gentle and kind, kindness himself, a people-person who really cares, and cares deeply, for people". She told of the incident when the waiter, Michael, was pouring your coffee and when he spilled it all over you how you made a joke of it to put him at ease. These words also came out of Marguerite's mouth, "even though he is taking this country down the river, he really cares and cares deeply for people." She wrote you a letter, the year of the election, opposing your views on abortion. And although she is a democrat from Helena, Arkansas she could not bring herself to vote that year.

At the end of our conversation, Marguerite mentioned she was leaving for Hope, to see relatives for a few days. And then she said "Hope is Bill Clintons home town." At that moment I suspected Hope would be the next stop on my travels.

Monmouth was decorated by Buzz Harper from New Orleans, the one and the same for whom you played your saxophone in his home. Regardless of the beautiful decor and beautiful setting of the grounds, it was now time to tear myself away from the plantation.

An anxious feeling about going to Hope came over me. I thought what better way to get to know William Jefferson Clinton than to walk the streets you walked and visit your friends and relatives. My every step was guided, and as I look back, it all started right before I entered the city of Hope.

Hope, Arkansas

It was evening and I thought I took a wrong turn. Just then, I noticed a police car following me. You know how you get the feeling you are going to be stopped? Deciding to stop to see if I really did miss my turn, Mr. policeman stopped also. He wanted to inform me I only had one headlight. He was very nice, so I decided to interview him on the spot.

"What do you think of Clinton?" I asked. Instead of answering, he asked me if I was going to the hospital, which I thought was an odd question. No, I said, and continued my questioning. He never did answer, however, he told me to go to the hospital and interview his wife, because she was better at this type of question. Since I was going there blind I thought, great, my first contact. The wrong turn I thought I made turned into a blessing. The deputy explained, that, if I stayed on this road, it was actually a shortcut.

The next morning, bright and early, I looked up the deputy's wife, Joy Jones, a very pretty young nurse. As I was interviewing Joy in the hospital lobby I noticed the gift shop directly in front of us. A little voice kept saying, "Go into the gift shop and talk to the ladies". Being obedient, I thanked Joy for her time and moseyed into the shop.

"I would like you to remember your original goals of why you wanted to be president. Everyone was so excited when you first became president, but now people are changing their minds. President Clinton, please remember what you are there to do."

Joy Jones

Inside I found three charming ladies, I introduced myself and began to ask questions. The name Bill Clinton stirred two of the ladies to chatter. One saying, "I wish they would leave him alone and let him do his job." The other lady said, "He is a good boy." The first lady continued, "Clinton is like my ex-husband, so charming, women will follow him out of town, I feel sorry for his wife." The third lady was dusting the shelves, she didn't have much to say. All of a sudden she turned, looked at me, and said, "Do you need a place to stay?" Without even thinking about it I heard myself give an enthusiastic "YES".

That afternoon I followed Evelyn Underwood home to her poultry ranch, a few miles out of town. Evelyn had recently lost her husband and was single-handedly managing her ranch. In a round-about-way, I have you to thank, for a dear friendship that has developed between us.

My new friend was immediately behind my research efforts. The way was totally prepared and laid out ahead of time. I was just going with the flow. Evelyn happened to be friends with your distant cousin, Gracie Collier Ross and her husband Burl, who lived right down the road. She gave them a call and before long I was sitting in their living room having a wonderful visit.

It was fascinating learning about your great Grandmother Edna Grisham, born April 19, 1878, living till August 8, 1952. Your great Grandfather, Lem Grisham, was born June 22, 1879 living till September 28, 1954. They said, "When you close your mouth and your chin sticks out, you are Lem all over." Burl described Edna as having big brown dancing eyes with beautiful little ringlets around her neck. He said you got your charisma from her.

8

I then learned of your Grandmother Edith Grisham Cassidy and your Grandfather Eldridge. As Gracie and Burl talked of the past it was as if they could see Edith wearing her little white hat with a flower on it as she sang in the choir. They told how your Grandparents and relatives used to cut loose singing at the Oak Grove Church. Burl said, "They were a real musical bunch." Thus, your musical roots.

Gracie and Burl Ross

Gracie invited me to the Oak Grove Church where several ladies quilt every Tuesday and have lunch. All the ladies brought a homemade dish of good southern cooking. They treated me to lunch and shared stories about you and Hope. It was a very special afternoon with Hattie Allen, Etta Collier, Irene Dodson, Wreath Jones, Doris Mullins, Carolyn Ross, Gracie Ross and my new friend Evelyn Underwood. I also met Ed Cooper who came by to pick up his mother-in-law, Hattie. Being an accomplished musician, the women talked him into playing the piano for us. Ed is also the author of "Farmers Paradise", maybe you have seen it, a book on the city of Hope and about you, Mr. President.

"You have fought the good fight, I pray when all is said and done you will rise victorious."

Gracie Ross

After lunch I took a walk through the cemetery beside the church and saw the resting place of your Grandparents and Great Grandparents. I noticed the marker, of your Aunt Ollie, who passed away February 3, 1990. Continuing to walk and read the headstones I wondered when you had last been there. I also visited Rose Hill Cemetery on RT 29. As I stood near your Mother's and Father's markers I felt as if I had gotten inside your soul just a bit. I'm sorry you never knew your birth Father. Your Heavenly Father is the only one that can fill that void.

Virginia Clinton Kelly
June 6, 1923 - January 6, 1994
William Jefferson Blythe
February 27, 1918 - May 17, 1946

"I will be a Father to you, and you will be my sons and daughters."
II Corinthians 6:18

Meanwhile I was enjoying my stay with Evelyn and the chickens. One day I went to the chicken house only to find her scooping up the baby chicks and putting them back over the divider they had escaped from. What else could I do but start chasing chickens with her. She felt sorry about having this city girl involved with those slippery, and I might add, fast little peeps. What Evelyn didn't know was, I am a country girl at heart. My Father had a farm for many years. My Aunt Esther and Aunt Hazel still have their farms in beautiful Pennsylvania.

By this time, I have discovered the Presidential Shop owned by Wayne and Elain Johnson. It is a very impressive collection of Presidential memorabilia. Elain was the perfect person to open this shop. As county coordinator, Elain had been around politics for sometime. She was and is a strong supporter of yours. She already had quite a collection of items, before the concept of a store was in the picture. Elain started selling t-shirts and hats from her office; they sold so fast she decided to put her own money into product. Soon the Presidential Shop was off and running.

Elain was one of the three hundred Arkansas Travelers that traveled the state as the FOB'S (friends of Bill). They would fly out of Little Rock and go to small towns where they would pick up vans and decorate them with Clinton signs. They were your mouthpiece to the local citizens as well as other politicians. Shiela Bronfman organized the FOB'S and I understand organized it was. Elain and her traveling partner, Sally Graves, were dedicated for the cause—getting you elected!

When I asked Elain to share a special memory concerning you, she immediately thought of the time she was at the Governors mansion. After a long days work she was waiting around with Ann McCoy, Ann's husband and Shiela, when you came along and said, "I don't know about you all but I'm going to the movies, anybody want to come?". Elain was flabbergasted, it remains a fun memory for her, going to a James Bond movie, with the then Governor Clinton.

As I was about to leave town, Elain said I should stay until Thursday because your Stepdad, Dick Kelly, and Jim Morgan, the author of your Mothers book "Leading from the Heart", would be at the Presidential Shop for a book signing appearance. I stayed and am glad I did .

Wayne and Elain had recently purchased the house on Thirteenth Street where you lived with your Mother as a young boy before moving to Hot Springs, Arkansas. In fact, when I drove into Hope, the first thing that caught my eye was the sign "CLINTON'S BOYHOOD HOME." Wayne said I was the first official visitor since they took it over. It was easy to picture you as a small boy running through the house as I went from room to room. As I stared into the backyard I could almost see you playing cowboys and Indians.

Southwestern Bell

Swbyp's℠

Hope

Bodcaw

Content Listing Inside

©Southwestern Bell Yellow Pages, Inc. 1993

June 1993–94

Area Code
501

BOYHOOD HOME of
BILL CLINTON

Not only is Hope an uplifting name for a town, but it also has 777 for its phone prefix. Seven is the number of completion in the Bible. The number seven appears 287 times in the Old Testament, the word "seventh" occurs 98 times.

Me

321 E 13th St.

12

The day of the book signing, Virginia Kelly's fans were there by the numbers. It was a great day for meeting family members and hearing stories of interest. Your cousin, Dale Drake, was a special lady that folks wanted me to meet. Just a few days before, she had an angina attack and was in the hospital. After a short stay she was discharged, she was determined to be at the Presidential Shop. She looked great; it was evident she was having a great time, however, I thought she was overdoing it a bit. She told me to call her in a day or two and we would get together; sorry to say the day I phoned she had just had another small attack. She has since gone to be with the Lord .

The only person I didn't get to meet was your Uncle Bud, his health was keeping him from having visitors. I understand that you were very close to him, his passing must have been a big loss. Though I didn't meet him I did enjoy meeting his daughter, Myra Grisham Irvin. She still stands out in my mind, as she looked stunning that day, wearing an orange top with shoes to match, her exceptional bronze tan not only set off her outfit but gave her a special glow. She shared some beautiful pictures of the Queens room from her recent stay at the White House.

One person that left a lasting impression after only a few minutes of conversation, was your Stepfather, Dick Kelly. His presence alone is powerful and has nothing to do with the fact that he is very tall and extremely handsome, well... maybe a little. My first thought was, "this is truly a man, a tower of strength." To my surprise, your Mother said in her book, that Dick was her "rock".

"A very favorite memory and one of my most enjoyable days was being in my working clothes at your three hundred and fifty guest black tie affair on St. Patricks Day."

Myra Grisham Irvin

Dick Kelly

Book Signing Day at The Presidential Shoppe

From left to right: Dale Drake, Dick Kelly, Jim Morgan
(I never claimed to be a photographer)

The Refurbishing of Bill Clintons First Home

Bill Clinton's first home (at 117 S Hervey) was owned by his grandparents, who kept Billy while his mother Virginia Kelly was studying medicine in New Orleans. Clinton lived in the house until he was four after Virginia remarried. She claimed Billy and moved to the other Clinton home at 321 E 13th St. Virginia before her death, helped the architectural firm of Cromwell and Associates in details of how the house looked in the 1940's.

Before   **After**

Courtesy of Clinton Birthplace Foundation

Jim Morgan had come all the way from Little Rock. He explained how you spent endless hours on the phone to help finish her book, "Leading from the Heart." It turned out very special, considering that your Mother did not live to see it completed. He is a gifted writer. When I started reading it, I couldn't put it down.

Those that love you really love you, they are devoted. A conversation I overheard concerning your other boyhood home, the one at 117 South Hervey Street, where you lived with your grandparents during your formative years, warmed my heart. What I heard went something like this, "The weeds were so bad around the house I couldn't stand it any longer, it was embarrassing. What would people think coming into Hope knowing this was one of the Presidents homes? My little boy and I go and mow the yard and try to keep the weeds pulled." To me this is a wonderful gesture for this mother and son to take it upon themselves to do what they can to make the place look as good as possible. Sorry I didn't get their names.

Since that time I have been back to Hope and found that that particular home has been completely refurbished and is quite beautiful. The wood frame house was built in 1917 and is now owned by the Clinton Birthplace Foundation. It is considered your first home and was placed on the National Register of Historic Places in 1994.

Oh yes, I also met your former secretary, Linda Dixon, now liaison between the White House and Little Rock. Let me just say she is very loyal to you, as she should be.

Do you remember Wilma Rowe Booker? She was the woman who helped deliver you at the hospital, and the first person to ever smack your butt. She showed me a great picture taken with you and some other friends from a few years ago. I ran into her at the old Union Pacific Railroad depot which is now the new Visitor Information Center.

Everyone in Hope was very friendly, however, when I met George Frazier, the Executive Director of the Clinton Birthplace Foundation, it was a definite highlight of my trip. We didn't have time to talk very long as he was headed to one of his many meetings, our brief time was very special. He made me feel like a longtime friend.

He sent this special memory:

April —

My wife, Effie, and I had the very great privilege of spending a night at the WhIte House some months ago and something happened there that to us illustrates the humanity and humility of Bill Clinton. When he returned to the White House about 9:00 PM after speaking at a dinner somewhere in the city, he joined us out on the Truman balcony. After sometime, in a break from discussing world problems and some personal stories, the President asked if we were hungry, stating that he had not had much of a chance to eat at the earlier dinner. Knowing that he would eat if we said "yes", he said he would see if there was some dessert left in their quarters. I expected him to press a button - or ring a bell- and ask one of the staff to check on the food. Instead, the President of the UnIted States, and surely one of the most pwerful men in the world, got up, went to Chelsea's room, got her up, and went to the kitchen. In just a few minutes they were back with a tray of delicious desserts which we all enjoyed.

In the course of our conversation that night, the President asked if we had obtained a copy of his mother's book, <u>Leading With My Heart</u>. We told him that we had not because it had not yet become available in Hope. He turned to Mrs. Carolyn Huber, who had joined us on the balcony, and who was our hostess for the visit, and told her to be sure we received a copy before we left for Hope tha next morning. The next morning, about 7:30 AM, there was a knock on our bedroom door. I OPened it and there stood the President of the UnIted States in his jogging clothes holding out his mother's book which he had personally autographed for us.

These are intimate memories of the man from Hope and I shall never forget them.

George Frazier

When it was time to leave Hope I followed Evelyn from the chicken ranch to Hot Springs Village where she had recently purchased a new home. We spent the day together and then she drove back to Hope and I went to Booneville, Arkansas to visit my Cousin Eddy Hine and his wife Ruth.

Hot Springs, Arkansas

After a few days I headed back to Hot Springs, not sure where I was going to start, since I didn't know anyone there. Of course I had met Dick Kelly, "the rock" and was hoping I could continue my interview with him, however, our schedules didn't mesh. As I was driving I was wondering if everything would fall into place as miraculously as it had in Hope. Here I was, now what?

Suddenly I noticed the race track. Since reading your Mothers book I realized this must be the same track she had talked about. Shortly down the road, I came upon a mall, I decided to stop and look around. Can you believe the first thing I came upon was the ARKANSAS MADE AND CLINTON AND GORE GALORE store! Jo Neil Marphew, the proprietor, was quite gracious and stood still for my questions. The subject of liberals came up. This was my chance to ask a question I had been curious about for some time. "What is your definition of a liberal," I asked. She told me she had given the liberal issue much thought and had decided the words to describe a liberal are, forgiving, tolerant, loving, not filled with hate, and in her mind she came to the conclusion that this equalled the same thing as being a Christian. What I just heard was a complete surprise to me. I think it would be safe to say that the conservatives would have a completely different definition. Now think about this, both the liberal and the conservative think of themselves as being the "good guys." Let me not get political just yet.

Jo and I also talked about Arkansas. She mentioned that the recession never touched there. I must admit I was impressed with the state of the state. It was not at all like your opponents made it out to be, when they said it was one of the poorest states in the country. It was clean, beautiful, organized and it seemed to be flourishing. The people are wonderful! Then there is the Tyson operation that provides many jobs. In fact, my new friend Evelyn was raising chickens for Tyson on her ranch in Hope.

Still at the mall some cookies caught my eye. As I was standing there deciding to have a cookie or not have a cookie I started talking to the owner, Jimmie House. He is not your biggest fan, however, he gave me my next contact. Jimmie first met you when you were governor. You came to give a speech for the grand opening of the new hospital where your Mother worked. Jimmies' job was to raise the flag. He has a hard time with your liberal agenda, especially wanting to lift the ban for homosexuals in the armed forces. As we were winding up our conversation he said I must meet Edith Irons. He told me where she lived and soon thereafter I bravely knocked on her door.

Normally I would phone first, but somehow I knew it would be okay. I enjoyed my interview with Edith so much I didn't want to see it end. She is delightful! Edith is one of your biggest supporters and absolutely loves you. Sometimes she would be telling me a story and she would stand up and act it out. She reenacted the time you went into her office, put your hands on your hips and said, "Where would you go to school if you wanted to be a foreign diplomat?" Her reply was, "Georgetown." She also made it quite clear that you would need to apply to at least three other schools as it may not be easy to get into Georgetown. You didn't, you decided right there and then it was going to be Georgetown. Your perserverance and determination have paid off time and again...your biography speaks for itself.

WILLIAM JEFFERSON CLINTON
BIOGRAPHY

1946, August 19 - William Jefferson Blythe IV born at Julia Chester Hospital in Hope, Arkansas. Attending Physician: Dr. Luther Lile. Mother Virginia Cassidy Blythe from Hope, Arkansas. Father. William J. Blythe III from Sherman, Texas. Father killed in car accident four months before Bill's birth.

1946 to 1950 - Bill lived with maternal grandparents Eldridge and Edith Grisham Cassidy at 117 South Hervey in Hope, Arkansas. Bill's mother, Virginia, trained as a nurse-anesthetist in Shreveport and New Orleans, Louisiana. Eldridge Cassidy owned and operated a small grocery store on North Hazel Street in Hope.

1950 - Virginia Cassidy married Roger Clinton, owner of the Buick dealership in Hope.

1950 to 1953 - Bill's family resided at 321 East 13th in Hope, Arkansas.

1951 to 1952 - Bill attended Mary Perkins' kindergarten on East Second Street in Hope.

1952 to 1953 - Bill attended first grade at Brookwood Public School in Hope.

1953, Summer - Bill's family moved to Hot Springs, Arkansas, where Roger Clinton worked for his brothers car dealership.

1960 to 1964 - In high school, Bill excelled in academics, school clubs, American Legion activities and band (he loves to play the saxophone). He also enjoyed golf, and would often caddy to earn extra spending money.

1961 - Bill took the Clinton name, at age 15.

1962 - Bill shook hands with President John F. Kennedy while attending an American Legion event in Washington, D.C.

1964 - Bill graduated from Hot Springs High School.

1968 - Graduated from Georgetown University.

1969 - Rhodes Scholar at Oxford University.

1971 - Graduated from Yale University Law School. Worked in Connecticut Senate campaign.

1972 - Worked in Texas for McGovern's presidential campaign.

1972 to 1976 - Taught law at the University of Arkansas.

1974 - Ran for Congress and lost against incumbent Republican Representative John Paul Hammerschmidt.

1975 - Married Hillary Rodham, a Wellesley and Yale Law School graduate from Park Ridge, Illinois.

1976 - Elected Attorney General of Arkansas.

1978 - Elected Governor of Arkansas. The youngest governor in the nation at the age of 32.

1980 - Daughter, Chelsea, was born in Little Rock on February 17.

1980 - Voted out of office, and began practicing law in Little Rock.

1982 - Re-elected Governor of Arkansas.

1983 - Received legislative approval for a comprehensive and nationally recognized education reform program.

1984 - Re-elected for third term as Governor

1986 - Re-elected for fourth term as Governor.

1986 to 1987 - Chairman, National Governors Association.

1986 to 1987 - Chairman, Education Commission of States.

1987 to 1988 - Represented nation's governors in working with Congress and White House to restructure nation's welfare.

1989 - Co-chair of Presidents Education Summit with Governors to draft National Education Goals.

1990 - Re-elected for the fifth term as Governor.

1991 - Received legislative approval for sweeping package of improvements in education, health, environment, highways and vocational-technical programs, tougher child support and domestic abuse laws, and tax cuts for low and middle income Arkansans.

1991, June - Fellow Governors rank Clinton as the Most Effective Governor in the country.

1991, July 17 - Announces two major manufacturing plant expansions in Hope, Arkansas, and tells media that Hope is a success model for rural industrial development. Since 1987, more new manufacturing jobs were created in Hope than any other rural city in the mid-south.

1991, October 3 - Announces candidacy for President of the United States. *"This is not just a campaign for the Presidency. It is a campaign for the future, for the forgotten hard-working middle class families of America who deserve a government that fights for them. A campaign to keep America strong at home and around the world". "We must forge a New Covenant of change that will honor middle-class values, restore the public trust, create a new sense of community, and make America work again. Together, we can make America great again, and build a community of hope that will inspire the world."*

1992, July - Nominated as Democratic Candidate for President.

1992, November 3 - Elected President of the United States.

1993, January 20 - Inaugurated as the 42nd President of the United States of America.

1996, November 5 - Elected to second term as President of the United States.

1997, January 20 - Inaugurated for second term as President of the United States.

Bill Clinton & John F. Kennedy
1962

President Clinton, from all I learned about you, there appears to be a missing link. From the time you were a young man with political aspirations to where you now sit in the White House something seems to have taken a different turn. Is it my imagination, or, was the good-intentioned-guy that shook President Kennedy's hand, greatly influenced by others?!

Edith glows, when she talks about you. She was proud about how you used to speak for different civic groups, and whatever the theme or subject, you could pull it off like a pro. What I found amazing is that at such a young age you always knew just the right thing to say and do. According to Edith, you never had to be told, you automatically knew.

Edith still remembers your exciting phone call, "Mrs. Irons, I got in" (Georgetown). You were fortunate to have her for a guidance counselor, in talking with her it was evident she really cared for her students. As she continued with the stories, I learned that you were very studious, in fact, your friends David and Caroline Leopoles used to remark, "Lets go over and watch Bill read." And then there was the interview for Georgetown. When they asked you how many languages you spoke, your answer, being "NONE", concerned your Mother just a bit. The schools question was, "What in the name of the Holy Father is a southern Baptist doing in the all Mother of Jesuit schools?" Your confident reply, to your mother was, "Don't worry, they'll know why I'm here after I've been here awhile." The day we spoke, Edith was in the process of planning a trip with your graduating class to the White House.

Edith also reminisced about your Mother. I was pleasantly surprised to find she was one of the Birthday Club girls I read about in Virginia's book. One day, Edith was driving in her car, missing your Mother terribly, she thought, "I was her best friend." Suddenly she put her foot on the brake, called herself an idiot and said , "Everybody was her best friend!" Virginia was a big loss to her. I only wish I could have had the privilege to have known this lady with the big heart and colorful personality.

Before I left, Edith took me for a drive to see a breathtaking view. It wasn't far from her house, I wish I could remember the name of the place. It was beautiful! Then she drove me by your home where you lived during your high school years, just a few blocks from her. Of course I wanted to see everything I could, so I ventured over to 1011 Park Avenue where you first lived after leaving Hope around 1954. It is a darling house, however, the sign in front, telling of it, being a former home of yours, is very small and not noticeable from the road. Maybe the owners prefer it that way so as not to have a lot of onlookers.

Just before the printing of this book I was saddened by the news that Edith passed away. She touched me so much. I was looking forward to visiting her again; we planned on going to her farm together in Mt. Ida, Arkansas. She had even offered me the downstairs room in her home to write this very book.

MRS. EDITH IRONS
Guidance Counselor

433 Oakwood
Hot Springs, Ark
7, 1913

Dearest Billy,

It is heartwarming and
a joy to see you on T.V.
each day with the Multitude
of faces filled with HOPE
as they listen to your plans
for the future of this great
Country! Knowing your
deep faith and convictions,
I truly believe you are
the "political Messiah" for
this Country at a critical time."
Remember our Love and
our prayers are with you always!
The people of Hot Springs and
Arkansas love, respect and
believe in you!

Sincerely
Edith Irons

Edith suggested I contact Virgil Spurlin, your high school band director. He was delighted to send this letter.

Hot Springs AR
June 2, 1998

President Bill Clinton
The White House
1600 Pennsylvania Ave.
Washington, D. C. 20500-2000

Dear Bill,

"School's out!" One more year, and, as a 37 year retiree of teaching, my mind goes back awhile when you were one of my "charges".

First of all, in this nostalgic tribute to you, I want to say that I am <u>so very proud</u> of you as our "fearless leader" of this wonderful country of ours! Your steps up the "ladder of success" have been steady and determined, starting out with those steps as a little boy, named "Billy", who, with Bible in hand, made his way down upper Park Ave. faithfully each Sunday morning to Sunday School and Church even tho' his mother could not always go with him because of her work as an anesthetist and nurse.

These steps continued on in matters of leadership and determination, sometimes not always in the easy way. You showed your true Christian-like attitude and character in all your dealings, no matter what, when, or where. You achieved so many outstanding feats in your teen years, your picture is on 30 pages in the 1964 "Old Gold Book", your Senior Yearbook.

Bill, we enjoyed those years together in BAND, didn't we! It was such an honor to have been your mentor and friend through it all.

I want you to know I'm still pulling for you and, with God as your guide I know that you will "Be all that you can be!" "Hang in there", buddy and may God continue to bless and guide you, is my prayer.

Your teacher and friend,

Virgil Spurlin
Virgil Spurlin

President Clinton, you were surrounded by love, though you never knew your Father you had a Grandfather for your role model. To this day your relatives are a big part of your life, so you know what family means. The one thing that impressed me most while reading "Leading From the Heart" was learning about your family meetings. When there was a major decision to be made, the three of you, Virginia, your brother Roger and yourself, would actually vote on the issue at hand. To me that is what family is all about, looking out for each others interest, caring.

Family Values

There is a lot of talk about family values and it amazes me how people actually don't agree on such a basic issue. What happened? In years past, most everyone was on the same wave length when it came to values and children. Morals and ethics were a given, now they have been turned into dirty words.

There are several factors that play a role in the moral breakdown of this country. The mass media has played a major part. Most people would agree the media is the single most influential factor in our society today. Knowing that, let me start with MTV. Of course you will always have to live down the question about your underwear. The lack of taste and respect that question posed is a small sampling of the condition of our country. My son is a grown man who likes to party a bit, and even he says it is too raw for him. Many are getting by with very distasteful projects in the name of "freedom of expression." Free speech never meant to remove common sense and decency. There used to be rules and codes to go by for film and television, no one called it censorship then.

There are three main reasons for the decline of morality in our films, TV, theatre, books, art, childrens cartoons and comic books. The downward spiral started when the church abandoned Hollywood. From 1933 to 1966 there was the influence and guidance of the Roman Catholic Legion of Decency and the Protestant Film office who developed the Motion Picture Code. The church offices insured that movies were wholesome and uplifting, that they did not denigrate the law or religion, and they did not lower the moral standards of the audience.

For financial reasons the office closed their doors in 1966. The shoes were now on different feet, the Gay and Lesbian Alliance Against Defamation, the Church of Satan, and other special interest groups moved in. The change was subtle, then again, most changes are. The previously used Motion Picture Code was not forced on the studios, they abided by it because movie producers recognized the high trust and confidence which was placed in them by the people of the world. Moreover, they recognized their responsibility to the public, knowing that entertainment and art are important influences in the life of a nation. With the new breed of power in place, the Motion Picture Code eventually went by the wayside.

The second reason stems from the introduction of cable TV. How many stations can we get now? It is exploding, especially with growing satellites and the information highway, the possibilities are endless when it comes to promoting good or evil. Cable has no regulations imposed on them the way the major networks do. I never understood that, still don't. Therefore, when a cable show pushes the envelope, NBC, CBS, ABC or the Fox network decide to ever so "subtly" step over the line just a little more. The more that children and adults are exposed to these influences, the more desensitized they become. That is one reason children are killing with out a sense of what is right or wrong.

The third is the breed of new writers. Many young people went into our universities with great hope for the future. However, they came out, and are coming out, as atheists with socialistic views. Many are venting their anger and frustrations from going through the educational system, where hope has been lost because no absolutes have been taught and America has been denigrated. Is it any wonder young people are confused?!

Many simply do not understand how susceptible children are to the messages that are put out there in every facet of entertainment. Years ago after seeing "Singing in the Rain" I wanted to be a "movie star", became obsessed with Hollywood and Debbie Reynolds was my constant role model. Fortunately, Debbie was the girl-next-door and set a good example to follow. How many girl and boy next-door-types do our children have for role models today? Many contemporary films aggravate teenage susceptibility leading them down a destructive path.

We keep pumping children and adults with the messages that violence is the way to solve problems. A United States Senate subcommittee, that you are probably familiar with, found that their is a direct correlation between violence on television and in movies and violent crime in every day life. According to the Children's Defense Fund teenage pregnancies have increased 500% since 1966, teenage abortions increased 1,100% since 1966, teenage sexually transmitted diseases 335%, teenage suicides increased 300% and of course guns in school were unheard of.

A few years ago, I started to take notice of small childrens' anger. Different times while shopping ,I would see little ones hitting there parents, downright defying them. Cuss words coming out of children's mouths who should be innocent. The children are out of control because of emulating what they see in the media, including so called childrens programming. They are watching programs that show defiance as being funny and accepted, the now-way of life. Rarely does a show display respect for the parent. Our childrens attitudes are evident of what we are all watching in our living rooms daily.

What ever seed is planted or conceived in the mind, whether it be good or evil, is what we will give birth to. What ever we put our attention on, is what we become. You have heard it said, "Garbage in, Garbage out"

Parents have been put in fear of disciplining their own children. It seems as if teachers are undermining the parents by telling children that their parents are stupid and that as children they have their rights. Students are being drilled about what goes on in the home, if a child says he has been spanked the parent is arrested for abuse. Mr. President what is going on? Where there are rules and discipline the child feels secure and loved. You, as a parent, must understand what I am saying. All evidence points to future government -control of our children.

Our young people are extremely confused by receiving mixed messages, ones they hear at school, those from the parents, their peers, the media and from the music that bombards their impressionable minds. Lyrics of today encourage sex, violence and suicide. These rock stars are their heroes and they follow their messages.

Not that many years ago, questionable language or any subject matter that denigrated the human condition was never an issue, it simply was bad taste and was not done. Today I am even hearing the Lord's name taken in vain on so called family programming and a lot of cursing on the radio as well. When it is heard on television and radio it is the same thing as saying it is okay to our young people. It is condoning it and helping to raise a country of disrespectful, foulmouthed citizens. Who loosened the reigns on the FCC?

President Clinton how about a COMMON SENSE AND DECENCY ACT? Of course, there are those that would shout CENSOR-

The rod and reproof give wisdom: but a child left to himself bringeth his mother to shame.

Proverbs 29:15

SHIP. To those I say wake up, we already have censorship. Special interest groups are managing their own censorship in Hollywood calling it "sensitivity."

A few years ago in the movie "Basic Instinct" the cast included an actor who played the part of a murderer who was a lesbian, the gay-rights-crowd didn't like it. They thought it made lesbians look bad. They demanded the right to make changes in the script. The film company refused. In retribution, gay activists disrupted the filming by throwing red paint, sounding car horns, and chanting obscene slogans.

Later another movie producer was looking for an actress to play the part of a lesbian who falls in love with a man. No actress would take the role for fear of offending lesbians and so bring on a new round of demonstrations. So this time the producer submitted the script to a gay media group and quietly made the changes that were demanded. Intimidation and scare tactics work even in Hollywood.

The film industry is going PC (politically correct). Here are a few examples.

Advocates for the disabled criticized the Peter Pan movie "Hook" for presenting a negative image of amputees.

A group called the National Stuttering Project complained about movies like the comedy "A Fish Called Wanda" for including characters who stutter.

When Disney decided to turn Jack London's classic novel, "White Fang" into a movie, animal rights groups reviewed the script. They persuaded Disney to tone down one scene where a wolf attacks a man and even include a disclaimer stating that healthy wolves do not attack humans.

When American Indian groups objected to the way "Dark Wind" portrayed their religious rituals, the producer changed the script.

Filmmakers balk when labeled POLITICALLY CORRECT, they prefer to call it, CULTURAL SENSITIVITY. When Christians have objected to certain negative portrayals of Jesus, the church or clergy were denounced as censors.

A few years back I was involved with a game show on a major network, the instructions for everyone right up-front were, "Do not mention God or say, thank you God," this is not the place. Sounds like censorship to me!

It wasn't that many years ago when Christians were the good guys. Good was good and bad was bad, it was cut and dry. Folks were hired for jobs if they were good, God-fearing people. Today, premarital sex, abortion, adultery, and lying are all glorified in the media. Some years ago those things that were considered shameless and downright evil were hidden underground. Today those same destroyers of a moral society have crawled to the surface, are glorified and deemed "okay" in the name of freedom. In fact, if someone opposes these sinful acts, they are labeled as right-wing fundamentalists, Nazis and even called dangerous.

The pendulum has swung! The Bible says in the last days good will appear as evil and evil will be accepted as good. Those that want to live by the traditional moral values this country was founded on, face persecution in their jobs and many times are refused employment because of their belief in God. Who would ever think that we would have seen this in the greatest country on Earth, where God was prevalent for two hundred years! The scholar that you are, you must know that when God's law is disregarded eventually the empire will crumble. Take a look around!

30

This has never been a Christian Nation!

Every evil is being protected by the Constitution under the guise of free speech yet the public is being stifled from expressing their beliefs, nativity scenes banned, schools no longer permitted to sing traditional Christmas carols. The word Christmas has been eliminated in the schools and many communities. Merry Christmas has been replaced by Happy Holiday banners. Satanic Bibles have been allowed on school desks but not the Holy Bible. Crosses are being taken off hillsides that were there for many decades because of the ACLU demanding it. The Ten Commandments are not allowed to hang on school walls, these are rules to live by, the Bible is the instruction manual for life. Without it there will be nothing but chaos, again, take a good look around!

The agenda of certain special interest groups is to reverse every moral law set forth in the Bible. While we go on with our busy lives many have barely noticed that it has already taken place.

Many people have no fear of God, instead, they mock His commandments, ridicule the Bible, make fun of all that is considered righteous and holy, and make themselves out to be God.

It boggles my mind when I hear someone say this has never been a Christian nation. All of history refers to our Christian heritage. In 1620 the Pilgrims established a government based on the Bible. The goal of government based on Scripture was further reaffirmed by individual colonies such as The Rhode Island Charter of 1683 which begins: "We submit our

Printed by permission from "Peter Green Design" Burbank, California.
Illustration by Peter Green

GOD'S LAWS

✝

The Ten Commandments

I Thou shalt have no other gods before me.

II Thou shalt not make unto thee any graven image.

III Thou shalt not take the name of the Lord thy God in vain

IV Remember the sabbath day, to keep it holy.

V Honour thy father and thy mother.

VI Thou shalt not kill.

VII Thou shalt not commit adultery.

VIII Thou shalt not steal.

IX Thou shalt not bear false witness against thy neighbour.

X Thou shalt not covet thy neighbour's house, thou shalt not covet thy neighbour's wife, nor his manservant, nor his maidservant nor his ox, nor his ass, nor any thing that is thy neighbour's.

THE SOVEREIGN LORD SAID,

"Judgement also will I lay to the line, and righteousness to the plummet."

ISAIAH 28:17

Printed by permission from the Plymouth Rock Foundation, Marlborough, New Hampshire.

The moral principles and precepts contained in the Scriptures ought to form the basis of all our civil constitutions and laws. All the miseries and evils which men suffer from vice, crime, ambition, injustice, oppression, slavery, and war, proceed from their despising or neglecting the precepts contained in the Bible.

Noah Webster

Bronze Plaque in Dirksen Office Building

persons, lives, and estates unto our Lord Jesus Christ, the King of kings and Lord of lords and to all those perfect and most absolute laws of His given us in His Holy Word." Those "absolute laws" became the basis of our Declaration of Independence, which includes in its first paragraph an appeal to the laws of nature and of nature's God. Our national Constitution established a republic upon the "absolute laws" of the Bible, not a democracy based on the changing whims of people.

Continuing through the decades of history, we find in the inaugural addresses of all the Presidents, and in the Constitution of all fifty of our states, without exception, references to the Almighty God of the universe, the Author and Sustainer of our liberty.

The Bible, through more than one hundred fifty years of early settlement in America, remained the base of her people's religious devotion, her education, and her government. The Bible sets the standard by which all moral judgments of life are to be measured and defines right from wrong.

Our legacy of liberty is firmly rooted in America's religious heritage. The Mayflower Compact of 1620, begins "In the Name of God", our national motto is, "In God we trust". Stop and think about that! Our motto is "In God we trust", yet the "powers that be," are hood winking the American public to believe that God has no place in the public arena.

Why, oh why, do we think we have been first among all nations? Because we are extra smart? No, because historically, we have placed God first in our national life. God has blessed America abundantly and prospered her people because of her abiding faith. Where the spirit of the Lord is, there is liberty. Without a moral, spiritually-based culture, freedom cannot survive.

It starts from the top down, Mr. President, from our rulers, from Washington, D.C. Our Supreme Court is ruling against the Creator of the universe. William Penn warned us, **"If we will not be governed by God, then we will be ruled by tyrants."** And George Washington proclaimed, **"It is impossible to govern the world without God and the Bible."** [1]

The first and almost the only Book deserving of universal attention is the Bible.

John Quincy Adams

The Bible is the one supreme source of revelation of the meaning of life, the nature of God and spiritual nature and need of men. It is the only guide of life which really leads the spirit in the way of peace and salvation.

Woodrow Wilson

All the good from the Saviour of the world is communicated through this Book; but for the Book we could not know right from wrong. All the things desirable to man are contained in it.

Abraham Lincoln

A thorough knowledge of the Bible is worth more than a college education.

Theodore Roosevelt

---

[1] The Bible: Rock of Our Republic — Page 97

The ACLU (American Civil Liberties Union) is one of the special interest groups that has helped bring down this country fast and furious. How did the ACLU get so much power? It was founded by prominent members of the Council on Foreign Relations (New World Order advocates), and the Communist Party of America. The ACLU was founded in 1920 by Felix Frankfurter, a CFR member; William Z. Foster, head of the US Communist Party at that time; Elizabeth Gurley Flynn, a Communist Party official; Dr. Harry F. Ward of Union Theological Seminary, a Communist fronter; and Roger Baldwin.

They claim to represent two hundred and forty million people. They provide free legal help to groups and individuals who, among other things, support legalized distribution of child pornography, promotion of homosexual and lesbian activities in the public schools, gay marriages, emancipation of children from parents, legalization of all narcotics, the removal of any expressions of religious faith in public life, and the demise of the tax exemption of churches plus mercy killings. It also supports dozens of other measures that would decriminalize most crimes.

Though I have seen some cases defended by the ACLU that were worthy, the percentage is very small compared to the ones that have eroded and corroded the very fabric of the greatest nation on earth.

On the next page you will see a typical letter circulated by the ACLU. Note the things they refer to as unconstitutional. Those of us on the other end of the spectrum believe they are the ones who are burning holes in our Constitution. Ironic isn't it?!

AMERICAN CIVIL LIBERTIES UNION

Dear Friend of Freedom:

A firestorm is sweeping across the country that threatens us all.

After more than a decade of organizing, the radical right now has real political power -- in Congress and in state legislatures and across the country. Their anti-liberties agenda has been endorsed by leading Republicans like Newt Gingrich and Bob Dole. And President Clinton has also capitulated to some of their demands.

In fact, a whole industry has sprung up in recent years solely to advocate and advance right-wing causes and explicitly to oppose the ACLU in courtrooms and in the public arena. There's the National Legal Foundation, the American Family Association Law Center, the Institute for Creation Research, the Western Center for Law and Religious Freedom, the Rutherford Institute, the American Spiritual Liberties Union, the U.S. Justice Foundation, and the Christian Educators' Association -- just to name a few!

This assault from the extreme right is unprecedented in both its scope and strategy. And it is particularly successful in advancing the unconstitutional religious agenda of the radical right. Prayer in public schools ... religious symbols on government property ... teaching the biblical story of creation as if it were science ... banning books ... censoring art, music and health information -- these are some of the legal challenges that are burning holes in our Constitution even as I write.

AND ... there is only one organization on the ground in every state -- responding to these challenges. That's the American Civil Liberties Union (ACLU). But frankly, as you can see on the enclosed map, we are stretched to our limits!

That's why I'm writing to urge you to become a member of the ACLU today. After 76 years of defending liberty, we know of only one way to guarantee that you can exercise your rights and freedoms when you need to: fight for them every time they're threatened.

The ACLU in Action:
A Fire Department for Your Endangered Rights

Together, we stand for tolerance, diversity and equality -- the uniquely American values expressed by our Bill of Rights. And together, we can fight to protect our rights today and to preserve them for future generations of Americans.

Don't sit on the sidelines while your rights go up in smoke. Join the ACLU and help us put out the fires that threaten to consume the Constitution.

Sincerely,

Ira Glasser
Executive Director

Foundation Grants

One might ask where their financial support comes from. It seems it comes from the same place other money comes from to influence the press, Congress and public policy — foundation grants. The ACLU is very well-heeled, operating with about a $15 million annual budget for the headquarters and approximately $10 million for its many affiliates through out the fifty states. Sources include the Playboy Foundation, Rockefeller, Carnegie, and Ford Foundations.

These figures are from a few years ago, think what they might be today.

The largest foundation on record is the Ford Foundation. It is very interesting how some of the Foundations money is spent:

- $1 million to the Council on Foreign Relations.

- $300,000 to study the influence of Communism in America, with Earl Browder, national secretary of the Communist party as a key staff member.

- $1,134,000 to the American Friends Service Committee to support a study of the Communist takeover of China.

The Ford Foundation has contributed millions of tax free grants to fund leftist and global initiatives, however, no grants are given for any religious purpose. Henry Ford Sr. would be turning over in his grave, the foundation policies have strayed so far to the left that Henry Ford II, grandson of the founder, resigned in disgust.

The second of the three largest foundations is the Rockefeller Foundation with billion dollar assets. In 1946 the report of the Rockefeller Foundation stated, "The challenge of the future is to make this one world." This fund has contributed faithfully to the CFR and its affiliate organizations. It also has been a training ground for future public servants.

The Carnegie Corporation known for the building of public libraries and technical colleges has shifted the use of some of their money to pro-Soviet initiatives.

These three foundations have over $10 billion in tax free wealth for the use of promoting propaganda to move us toward a one world government and world socialism.

School Prayer

Just a few years later, 1963, we allowed a registered communist to take prayer out of school. Madalyn Murray O'Hair an atheist involved with the Socialist Workers Party, the Socialist Labor Party, and the Communist Party, one woman with this background helped to destroy our sacred value system.

On June 25, 1962 the Supreme Court declared prayer in the schools unconstitutional. Senator Robert Byrd of West Virginia was so moved by the disastrous decision that two days later he delivered an address to his colleagues in Congress reminding them of the Christian symbolism throughout their own city. He escorted them to the Library of Congress, the Washington Monument, the Lincoln Memorial, the Jefferson Memorial, the Supreme Court, and other landmarks. As he concluded he said:

> "Inasmuch as our greatest leaders have shown no doubt about God's proper place in the American birthright, can we, in our day, dare do less?"

Senator Byrd also cited these words of Jefferson:

> "TO REMOVE GOD FROM THIS
> COUNTRY WILL DESTROY IT."

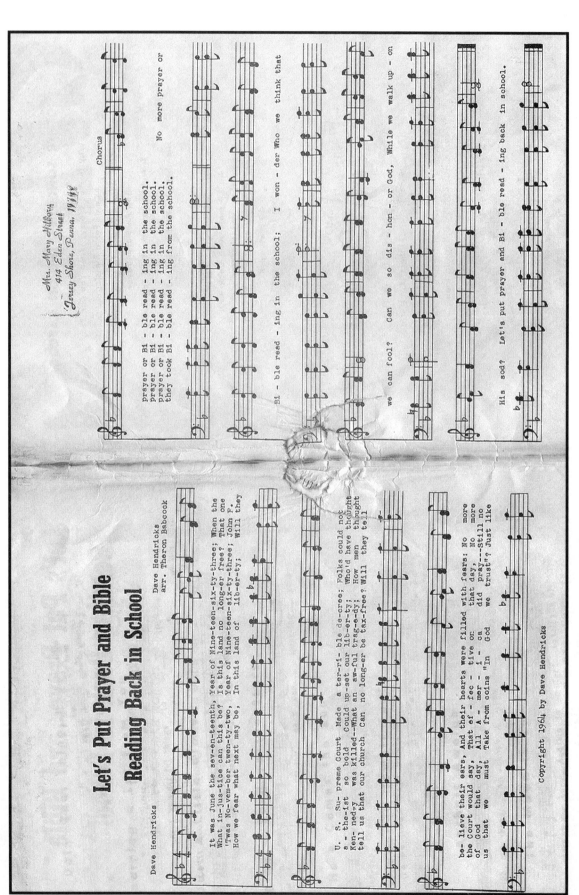

This song sheet, which went through the 1972 flood in Pennsylvania was found among my grandmother's belongings.

Congressional Record

United States of America

PROCEEDINGS AND DEBATES OF THE *104th* CONGRESS, FIRST SESSION

MONDAY, FEBRUARY 6, 1995

Senate

VOLUNTARY SCHOOL PRAYER: IT MUST BE RESTORED

Mr. HELMS. Mr. President, the U.S. Senate, since the inception of the 104th Congress, has thus far participated in two significant debates. The first determined the role of the Federal Government in the affairs of the States; and the second will decide whether, after decades of insane spending of the American taxpayers' money, the U.S. Congress will finally get around to controlling itself with a balanced budget amendment to the U.S. Constitution.

All of us should recognize the importance of these significant issues. Certainly, I do. However, one wonders whether liberal politicians. Who time after time have beaten back attempts to restore moral and spiritual principles to our society, are not content for Congress to focus its attention on the Nation's economic woes while spiritual issues-for example, protecting unborn life and restoring school prayer are being sidetracked with harsh rhetoric such as extreme, worthless, and insignificant.

Mr. President, lest our leftward-tilted friends become too satisfied with the neglect of religious and spiritual values in America, they should be reminded of what our Nation's first President acknowledged and what so many in Congress have disregarded that our Nation's material and spiritual wealth is bestowed by the Creator only when we seek His audience in our Nation's affairs George Washington stated:

*** the propitious smiles of heaven can never be expected on a nation which disregards the eternal rules of order and right which heaven itself has ordained.

Mr. President, in 1962, the Supreme Court forfeited by judicial fiat the rights of millions of American children to invoke in their schools the blessings and guidance of God. Consequently, this act begat a popular culture, the values, discipline, and moral standards of which are devoid of God and laden with relativism A greater crime against our children could hardly be conceived.

Today, all of us should take note of the desperate need to return to our Nation's children their constitutional right to voluntary prayer in the public schools. In this regard, a guest column published by the Charlotte (N.C.) Observer and authored by Dr. Norman Geisler, dean of Southern Evangelical Seminary in Charlotte, NC, is very worthy of broad consideration. Dr. Geisler titled it "10 Reasons for Voluntary School Prayer."

Dr. Geisler is a foremost theologian as evidenced by his impressive catalog of degrees and achievements. He has lectured and traveled in 50 States and 24 countries on 6 continents. Dr. Geisler has been honored and listed in many leading publications including "The Who's Who in Religion," The Writers Who's Who," and "Men of Achievement." He has authored or coauthored 45 books on a wide range of social, moral, and religious issues.

Mr. President, I fervently hope that all Senators will spend a few minutes reading Dr. Geisler's convincing defense of the right of children to pray in public schools. His defense of one of our Founding Father's rules of heaven has never been more needed nor more eloquently stated.

I ask unanimous consent, Mr. President that the January 30 guest column in the Charlotte Observer, "10 Reasons for Voluntary School Prayer," be printed in the RECORD.

(From the Charlotte Observer, Jan. 30, 1995)

10 REASONS FOR
VOLUNTARY SCHOOL PRAYER

(By Norman L. Geisler)

There are many good reasons for a constitutional amendment to permit voluntary prayer in the public schools. Ten come to mind.

1. Our government was based on religious principles from the very beginning: The Declaration of Independence says: 'We hold these truths to be self-evident, that all men are created equal, that they are endowed by God with certain unalienable rights — Indeed, it speaks of God, creation, God-given moral rights, the providence of God and a final Day of Judgment all of which are religious teachings. Indeed, the Supreme Court affirmed (Zorach, 1952) that "We are a religious people whose institutions presuppose a Supreme Being." And school prayer has been an important part of our religious experience from the very beginning.

2. The First Amendment does not separate God and government but actually encourages religion. It reads: "Congress shall make no law respecting the establishment of religion, nor prohibiting the free exercise thereof." The first clause merely declares that the federal government cannot establish one religion for all the people. It says nothing about "separation of church and state." In fact, five of the 13 states that ratified it had their own state religions at the time. The second clause insists that the government should do nothing, to discourage religion. But forbidding prayer in schools discourages religion.

3. Early congressional actions encouraged religion in public schools. For example, the Northwest Treaty (1787 and 1789) declared: "Religion, morality, and knowledge being necessary for good government and the happiness of mankind, schools and the means of learning shall forever be encouraged." Thus, religion, which includes prayer, was deemed to be necessary.

PRESIDENTS ENCOURAGED PRAYER

4. Early presidents, with congressional approval, made proclamations encouraging public prayer. President Washington on Oct. 3, 1789, declared: "Whereas it is the duty of all nations to acknowledge the providence of Almighty God, to obey His will, to be grateful for His benefits, and humbly to implore His protection and favour, and Whereas both Houses of Congress have, by their joint committee, requested me to recommend to the people of the United States a day of public thanksgiving and prayer…

5. Congress has prayed at the opening of every

session since the very beginning. Indeed, in a moment of crisis at the very first Continental Congress Benjamin Franklin urged prayer and observed that "In the beginning of the Contest with Great Britain, when we were sensible to danger we had daily prayer in this room for Divine protection. Our prayers, Sir, were heard, & they were graciously answered. ... And have we now forgotten that powerful Friend? or do we imagine we no longer need His assistance? ... I therefore beg leave to move that henceforth prayer imploring the assistance of Heaven, and its blessing on our deliberations, be held in this Assembly every morning before we proceed to business, and that one or more of the clergy of this city be requested to officiate in that service." Congress has begun with prayer ever since. If the government can pray in their sessions, why can't the governed pray in their (school) sessions?

6. Public schools had prayer for nearly 200 years before the Supreme Court ruled that state-mandated class prayers were unconstitutional (Engel, 1962). The fact that prayer was practiced for nearly 200 years establishes it by precedent as a valid and beneficial practice in our schools.

7. Since the court outlawed prayer, the nation has been in steady moral decline. Former Secretary of Education William Bennett revealed in his cultural indexes that between 1960 and 1990 there was a steady moral decline. During this period divorce doubled, teenage pregnancy went up 200%, teen suicide increased 300%, child abuse reached an all time high, violent crime went up 500% and abortion increased 1000%. There is a strong, correlation between the expulsion of prayer from our schools and the decline in morality.

8. Morals must be taught, and they cannot properly be taught without religion. There cannot be a moral law without a moral Law Giver. And there is no motivation for keeping the moral law unless there is a moral Law Giver who can enforce it by rewards and punishments.

SECULAR HUMANISM ESTABLISHED

9. Forbidding prayer and other religious expressions in public schools establishes, in effect, the religion of secularism.
   The Supreme Court has affirmed that there are religions, such as "secular humanism" which do not believe in God (Torcaso, 1961). Justice Potter (Abington, 1963) rightly feared that purging the schools of all religious beliefs and practices would lead to the "establishment of a religion of secularism" In fact, the beliefs of secular humanism are just the opposite of the Declaration of Independence. By not allowing theistic religious expressions, the courts have favored the religious beliefs of secular humanism, namely, no belief in God, God-given moral laws, prayer and a Day of Judgement.

10. To forbid the majority the right to pray because the minority object, is to impose the irreligion of the minority on the religious majority. Forbidding prayer in schools, which a three-quarters majority of Americans favors, is the tyranny of the minority. It is minority rule, not democracy. Why should an irreligious minority dictate what the majority can do? The majority wishes to preserve our moral and spiritual values and, thus, our good nation.

Mr. President why do you think the Supreme Court declared prayer in the schools unconstitutional? How did that happen in the land of the free (speech)? Why was an important issue such as this not put to a public vote? Why are most issues not put to a public vote? When some bills are put to a vote they are worded in such a way as to confuse the voter, a person may think they are voting against something when in fact they are voting for it. What exactly happened to the "majority rules?"

I'm pleased to report that the small boy, William J. Murray, who was used to take prayer out of school is now a passionate advocate for the restoration of prayer in public schools. His book "Let Us Pray" should be read by all, it once and for all clarifies the issue of school prayer in America. If you ever run across his life story "My Life Without God" I also recommend this most fascinating book. One could not read these writings without realizing that the banning of prayer was a horrific measure and a great destroyer of good in this country.

President Clinton, several years ago someone said to me that Americans were receiving propaganda from our own government, well, I would not hear of this or begin to believe it. While serving as the Los Angeles press contact for the Pat Robertson Presidential campaign, I started to become politically savvy. The more I learned the more I found it to be true after all.

To a naive American who thought that everything our government did was for the good of the country and it's people, how devastating to find out differently. At first there was anger, then I wanted to be Miss fixit. When I found out I couldn't change the world I was frustrated, my stomach would become queasy. Tears would well up in my eyes just thinking about the times I had wept at the passing of an American flag in a parade. There are a number of emotions most Americans are experiencing, the biggest seems to be frustration and helplessness.

I believe most politicians start out with good intentions, however, when they find out how the system truly operates they too must have their moments of great disappointment. The propaganda is working! Many folks who had definite traditional opinions have been swayed by the way information has been presented in the media.

A good example of this is Dr. Kervorkian. When he first came on the scene people were appalled at the thought of assisting people in dying, however, after a few times of hearing of his assisted suicides it started to become old news. Many started thinking that perhaps mercy killing is a compassionate way of dealing with ill and sometimes even depressed people. The more a person is exposed to anything the more they are desensitized.

Speaking of the media, well maybe I won't, most of us know it is controlled, Amen!

You must feel the peoples frustrations, their opinion does not seem to count. Again, they are feeling helpless and angry at watching America disintegrate before their eyes. Mr. President, you are heard talking about what is good for the American people, yet, are you letting the American people decide for themselves? The government is out of control. More freedoms are stripped of it's citizens daily. No small wonder we have militia's forming throughout the country. They know what is coming and are prepared to die for their freedom. Of course, the media portrays them as dangerous, when in fact, most of them are men who fought for this country and are ready to do it again. Though I understand it I am not condoning it. Read this profound article on the militant movement.[2]

As a child I remember my Grandmother telling me that one day this would no longer be America, that communists were infiltrating our government. She also said there will not have to be a war between the United States and the Communists because they are going to take over so subtly we won't even know how it happened. My Grandmother was never wrong!

[2] The Elijah Report: Militant Patriot Movement — Page 105

44

When the righteous are in authority the people rejoice; but when the wicked rule the people mourn

Proverbs 29:2

In October of 1993, you called several pastors together for a breakfast meeting at the White House. Many of those pastors have taken a great deal of flack, some for just attending, others for not confronting you on spiritual issues. That breakfast meeting was the topic of conversation for some time.[3]

Christians across the land are standing in the gap for you with their heartfelt prayers. I truly believe you are the most prayed for President that ever sat in the White House. Please forgive those Christians that are spewing hate instead of praying. Many people that profess to be Christians have the head knowledge of the Bible, and not the love of Jesus in their heart.

President Clinton, you must have a spiritual tug-of-war going on inside of you. Many times I believe you go against what you know to be the truth because you truly do not have a choice. Dale Evans said "Clinton is in over his head", I tend to agree. Some, reading this, will not have a clue of what I'm talking about. I often wonder if you are aware of what you are doing each time you sell a little more of America to the enemy (devil), let alone what you are doing to your own soul. Wow! That is a strong statement, I'm going to let it stand. Keep reading!

When I watched the tears flow from your eyes as you listened to the song Amazing Grace, I knew God was at work in your life. When God begins a good work in us, he is faithful to complete it. You are a work in progress by your Heavenly Father, as all of us

[3] Breakfast Meeting Report: Standing in the Gap — Page 111

are that believe. Like any Daddy who loves His children he chastises them when they are not obedient. This process is necessary to grow us up in Him so we can become Christ-like to be able to fulfill our calling. You may think your calling is to be President. As worthy as that position is, there is still a higher calling.

Thank the Lord we are under his grace.

Grace (grās), —n. 1. good will, favor. 2. the favor and love of God: *fall from grace*. 3. mercy or pardon. 4. favor shown by granting a delay.

Taken from the *Thorndike Barnhardt Dictionary*, 1973

It would be a heroic gesture for you to hold a town hall meeting for the Christian community. As President (in or out of office) you could take a stand and help stop the persecution against the church. Or do you really not have a choice, just as you said you did not have a choice when it came to vetoing the bill against partial birth abortion?

Have you seen the procedure for the partial birth abortion? If you see it you cannot deny that it is plain murder. There does not need to be legislation for abortion for the safety of the Mother, any doctor would automatically do what is best for the Mother if there is a life threatening situation. There is no difference between partial birth abortion or killing the baby after delivery. If you do not believe this I suggest you check it out for yourself, you may have been given very misguided information.

If this article below has been accurately reported, I would like to know what you were thinking.

"God Will Hold You To Account, Mr. President"

AFA ACTION ALERT
American Family Association, Inc.
Dr. Donald E. Wildmon, President - Post Office Drawer 2440, Tupelo, Mississippi 38803
Telephone: 601/844-5036; Fax: 601/844-9176
Email: bud@afa.net; World Wide Web: http//www.afa.net

Just last week, Matthew Schenck, the teenage son of our good friend, Reverend Robert Schenck. General Secretary to the National Clergy Council, was lamenting that nothing exciting, ever seemed to happen. That was then. This is now. On Christmas Eve, your editor invited a small group of friends, including the Schenck family, to a service at Washington's National Cathedral, which was also attended by the President and his family. The service provided a rare opportunity to share a few words with the Churchgoer-in-Chief, and as we made our way up to communion, several people offered him Christmas greetings.

Concerned for the President's spiritual well-being, Reverend Schenck's Christmas gift was in the form of eight well-chosen words. In a scriptural admonition referring to the President's veto of the partial birth abortion ban, he said quietly and respectfully: "God will hold you to account, Mr. President."

The President appeared shocked at hearing this truth and activated his eager Secret Service. As the choir made their way down the center aisle singing "What Child Is This", the Reverend was accosted and prevented from leaving the Cathedral. One Secret Service agent reached inside the minister's jacket, pulled out his wallet and started rifling through it in a 15-minute spectacle which left eyewitnesses, including your editor, wondering whether they had been suddenly transported not to Bethlehem but to Beijing. The Secret Service apparently observe no boundaries once they decide, in their own unique interpretation of reality, that the President's life is threatened. By the time we left the Cathedral, the Reverend's Drivers License had not been returned, and out on Wisconsin Avenue, eight members of the Secret Service, having taken a shortcut, blocked the sidewalk in a tactic your editor had not seen since a 1981 visit to Moscow.

This was neither Beijing nor Moscow but Washington. Capital of the Free World, yet these actions were those of a paranoid regime in an advanced stage of terminal decay, reminiscent of the final days of the Soviet Union. If the President feels threatened by God's word, it is not because his life is under threat, but because his Eternal Life is under threat, and that is beyond the jurisdiction even of the Secret Service.

The White House refused to acknowledge that these events had taken place. Would they say that planting three rows of black people immediately behind the President was a coincidence? It is an insult to anyone to be used as a stage prop. It has often been reported that President Clinton is a showman who lacks substance. These events witnessed with our own eyes support that theory and also illustrate his ruthlessness. If this was his reaction to a scripture, can one imagine what he does to someone who really threatens his political or physical life? The Reverend was right: in His own perfect time, God will hold Bill Clinton, and all of us, to account for what we do and for what we fail to do.[4]

Following the publication of this week's Update, the Secret Service stated they had acted appropriately. Here is Reverend Robert Schenck's response to them:

Statement By The Reverend Robert Schenck, General Secretary to the National Clergy Council

Friday, December 27, 1996

The Secret Service have today described their actions in accosting and detaining me during a Christmas Eve service at Washington National Cathedral as "appropriate". I beg to differ.

President Clinton describes himself as a Christian and certainly enjoys being seen frequently with a Bible in his hand. The Scriptures tell us that: "If someone is caught in a sin, you who are spiritual should restore him gently" (Galatians 6: 1). That is precisely what I was doing. Reminding the President that he is accountable to God is nothing more nor less than the truth.

Indeed, as has been pointed out in the media, the Pope, Mother Teresa and Billy Graham have rebuked the President for his actions. Would the Secret Service treat them in the same way as they treated me?

The Secret Service have no business interfering in matters between two brothers in Christ, especially inside a church and during a service, assuming that President Clinton is sincere about his Christian faith.

As Exegesis pointed out in their Update of today's date: "If the President feels threatened by Gods word, it is not because his life is under threat, but because his Eternal Life is under threat, and that is beyond the jurisdiction even of the Secret Service."

You may contact President Clinton by email at the following:

president@whitehouse.gov

Printed by permission from American Family Association, Tupelo, Mississippi.

---

[4] Biblical Principles: Accountability — Page 115

48

Mother Teresa decried the evil of abortion at the National Prayer Breakfast in Washington, D. C. on Feburary 3, 1994, as President Bill Clinton and wife Hillary, left, and Vice-President Al Gore and wife Tipper, right look on.

Mother Teresa's speech in its entirety

WHATEVER YOU DID UNTO ONE OF THE LEAST, YOU DID UNTO ME
Mother Teresa of Calcutta

On the last day, Jesus will say to those on His right hand, "Come, enter the Kingdom. For I was hungry and you gave me food, I was thirsty and you gave me drink, I was sick and you visited me." Then Jesus will turn to those on His left hand and say, "Depart from me because I was hungry and you did not feed me, I was thirsty and you did not give me to drink, I was sick and you did not visit me." These will ask Him, "When did we see You hungry, or thirsty or sick and did not come to Your help?" And Jesus will answer them, "Whatever you neglected to do unto one of the least of these, you neglected to do unto Me!"

As we have gathered here to pray together, I think it will be beautiful if we begin with a prayer that expresses very well what Jesus wants us to do for the least. St. Francis of Assisi understood very well these words of Jesus and His life is very well expressed by a prayer. And this prayer, which we say every day after Holy Communion, always surprises me very much, because it is very fitting for each one of us. And I always wonder whether 800 years ago when St. Francis lived, they had the same difficulties that we have today. I think that some of you already have this prayer of peace - so we will pray it together.

Let us thank God for the opportunity He has given us today to have come here to pray together. We have come here especially to pray for peace, joy and love. We are reminded that Jesus came to bring the good news to the poor. He had told us what is that good news when He said: "My peace I leave with you, My peace I give unto you." He came not to give the peace of the world which is only that we don't bother each other. He came to give the peace of heart which comes from loving - from doing good to others.

And God loved the world so much that He gave His son - it was a giving. God gave His son to the Virgin Mary, and what did she do with Him? As soon as Jesus came into Mary's life, immediately she went in haste to give that good news. And as she came into the house of her cousin, Elizabeth, Scripture tells us that the unborn child - the child in the womb of Elizabeth - leapt with joy. While still in the womb of Mary - Jesus brought peace to John the Baptist who leapt for joy in the womb of Elizabeth.

And as if that were not enough, as if it were not enough that God the Son should become one

(Continued on page 119)

STATE OF ARKANSAS
OFFICE OF THE GOVERNOR
State Capitol
Little Rock 72201

Bill Clinton
Governor

September 26, 1986

Arkansas Right To Life
P.O. Box 1697
Little Rock, AR 72203

Dear Mrs.

Thank you for giving me the opportunity to respond to the
Arkansas Right to Life Questionnaire. However, most of the
questions address federal issues outside the authority of a
governor or the state.

Because many of the questions do concern the issue of
abortion, I would like for your members to be informed of my
position on the state's responsibility in that area. I am
opposed to abortion and to government funding of abortions.
We should not spend state funds on abortions because so
many people believe abortion is wrong. I do support the
concept of the proposed Arkansas Constitutional Amendment
65 and agree with its stated purpose. As I have said, I am
concerned that some questions about the amendment's impact
appear to remain unanswered.

Again, thank you for allowing me to share my position on
this important issue.

Sincerely,

Bill Clinton
Bill Clinton

BC:kt

Please tell me why Christians are being ridiculed for trying to hang on to this country's Christian heritage. The values at stake are not being forced on anyone, these values have always been what ruled every part of our society. When good folks see these values being stripped from our children, that is good cause to stand up and fight to keep what has always been sacred. Where these basic good book rules are applied you see integrity, where they are lacking you see unrest. I mentioned prayer being taken out of school; when there was Bible reading and prayer to start the school day, there were no guns, no theft to speak of. If one girl got pregnant it was a scandal. What you did have was respect for the teachers, orderly classrooms and children could read when they graduated.

And Mr. President why do we all of a sudden need reading facilitators. All we have to do is put phonetics back in the hands of the teachers. It used to be that everyone learned to read in first grade, it was so basic we learned it and went on with school. Phonics is the answer and most everyone recognizes that is what is needed.

Why, when the answer to something is so simple is it overlooked and so difficult to put in place? First of all why would phonics be eliminated when it worked and every student was reading? Second of all why would phonics not be put back as soon as it was discovered children were not learning to read? Can anyone answer these questions?

My niece, Adina, and nephew, Aron, attend a Christian school and guess what, they can read and they are in a safe environment. Does this not prove this Ten Commandment teaching handles the problem of crime and all the other problems that politicians claim they want to fix. Even if a person is not a believer, if prayer and Bible reading fix the problems, why does it so anger people?

Gang members have been turned around by churches because pastors have taken the time to get involved in their lives by loving them and telling them about the Word of God. If God is eliminated from this country as the ACLU and others are trying to do, you will see evil abound. You think it is bad now, you haven't seen anything yet! Catholics, Jews and Protestants agree on the importance of keeping this nation sovereign — ONE NATION UNDER GOD.

Myth of Church and State

Where was the separation of church and state years ago? Do these special interest groups all of a sudden know what our forefathers really meant? You know, as well as most Americans, that there is no such thing as "separation of church and state". God was placed in every aspect of government and our schools by men who knew God and knew the importance of letting God reign. Our first text book in this country was the Bible. It would surprise most people to learn that Yale, Princeton, Harvard and most every Ivy League school was founded by clergy and were established primarily to train ministers of the gospel.[5]

The biggest lie of this century is the "separation of church and state," which has been accepted by many Americans because it has been brought about by intimidation. The ACLU instills fear with the threat of law suits. The U.S. Constitution does not use the phrase "wall of separation" anywhere. That phrase was used in 1802 by Thomas Jefferson and his meaning was that government should not have control over the church or religion.

The first Chief Justice of the United States Supreme Court, John Jay, wrote, "Providence has given to our people of their rulers, and it is the duty of a Christian nation to select and prefer Christians for their rulers." Neither American history nor the scrip-

---

[5] The History of America's Education — Page 125

tures support the idea of the First Amendment being interpreted to keep the church out of politics as it is used today. It was written to keep the government from establishing a state church, like the Church of England.

It's difficult for me to comprehend why some people are so blinded to the fact that when "separation of church and state" went into effect it's driving force brought in the abortion holocaust, failure of the public educational system, higher crime rate, lower media standards, children with foul mouths and no manners, need I go on! As I may have mentioned, God's hand was removed and it allowed Satan to come in and have a party.

For those reading this that are not aware of "crisis management" let me say this about that — again the "powers that be" make a problem so they can fix it. All the lowering of the standards in this country have been brought about on purpose. When things get so bad that the country and it's people are out of control, near destruction, that is when the Antichrist will step in and be the saviour. People will be so elated that someone is going to make everything "all better" that they will go along with the beast (666) believing he is Christ. DO NOT BE DECEIVED!

Because of the "crisis management" we have less and less freedom. When a disaster takes place, immediately there is a new bill passed in the name of safety when in reality it is just a way to take more control. I could go on and on about how our every move and conversation is being monitored, however, as it is, some will think I'm paranoid. For those I say, do your homework.

Most people laugh at the word conspiracy; however, the "powers that be" need to dumb down America in order to take control of the masses. They also need to strip God from the country because they know that followers of Jesus Christ will not follow the coming Antichrist. If a country's people are uneducated and spiritually unenlightened, they will succumb to the whims of the government and do what ever they are told.

A short excerpt from the celebrated sermon that follows was preached in London on November 4, 1789, during the 101st anniversary of the American Revolution, by Richard Price. He was born at Tynton in Glamorganshire, Wales, and gained fame as a supporter of the American and French revolutions. A friend of Benjamin Franklin, he was a Presbyterian minister and moral philosopher. Read these wise words as to what Price had to say.

Virtue-and Liberty. These are, therefore, the blessings in the possession of which the interest of our country lies, and to the attainment of which our love of it ought to direct our endeavours. By the diffusion of knowledge it must be distinguished from a country of barbarians: by the practice of religious virtue, it must be distinguished from a country of gamblers, atheists, and libertines: and by the possession of liberty, it must be distinguished from a country of slaves. I will dwell for a few moments on each of these heads:

Our first concern, as lovers of our country, must be to enlighten it. Why are the nations of the world so patient under despotism? Why do they crouch to tyrants, and submit to be treated as if they were a herd of cattle? Is it not because they are kept in darkness, and want knowledge? Enlighten them and you will elevate them. Shew them they are men, and they will act like men. Give them just ideas of civil government, and let them know that it is an expedient for gaining protection against injury and defending their rights, and it will be impossible for them to submit to governments which, like most of those now in the world, are usurpations on the rights of men, and little better than contrivances for enabling the few to oppress the many. Convince them that the Deity is a righteous and benevolent as well as omnipotent Being, who regards with equal eye all his creatures, and connects his favour with nothing but an honest desire to know and do his will; and that zeal for mystical doctrines which has led men to hate and harass one another, will be exterminated. Set religion before them as a rational service, consisting not in any rites and ceremonies, but in worshipping God with a pure heart, and practising righteousness from the fear of his displeasure and the apprehension of a future righteous judgment, and that gloomy and cruel superstition will be abolished, which has hitherto gone under the name of religion, and to the support of which civil government has been perverted. Ignorance is the parent of bigotry, intolerance, persecution and slavery. Inform and instruct mankind, and these evils will be excluded. Happy is the person who, himself raised above vulgar errors, is conscious of having aimed at giving mankind this instruction. Happy is the scholar or philosopher who at the close of life can reflect that he has made this use of his learning and abilities: but happier far must he be, if at the same time he has reason to believe he has been successful, and actually contributed, by his instructions, to disseminate among his fellow-creatures just notions of themselves, of their rights, of religion, and the nature and end of civil government. Such were Milton, Locke, Sidney, Hoadly, &c. in this country, such were Montesquieu, Fenelon, Turgot, &c. in France. They sowed a seed which has since taken root, and is now growing up to a glorious harvest. To the information they conveyed by their writings we owe those revolutions in which every friend to mankind is now exulting. What an encouragement is this to us all in our endeavours to enlighten the world? Every degree of illumination which we can communicate must do the greatest good. It helps to prepare the minds of men for the recovery of their rights, and hastens the overthrow of priest-craft and tyranny. In short, we may, in this instance, learn our duty from the conduct of the oppressors of the world. They know that light is hostile to them, and therefore they labour to keep men in the dark. With this intention they have appointed licensers of the press; and, in popish countries, prohibited the reading of the Bible. Remove the darkness in which they envelope the world, and their usurpations will be exposed, their power will be subverted, and the world emancipated.

Prayer Window, U.S. Capitol

It will take a committed man of God in complete obedience to the Holy Spirit to stand up and denounce the myth of "church and state". Not even the senators and congressmen who know the truth are speaking out to turn this fallacy around. Of course if you did take a stand on this issue you would not be popular with everyone, especially the people you have surrounded yourself with. However, I'll tell you what would happen. Mainstream America would stand up and cheer you! I can only imagine how this country would be blessed (once again) if we had a President who took his orders from almighty God. From whom do you take your orders?

The Eighty-third Congress set aside a small room in the Capitol, just off the rotunda, for the private prayer and meditation of members of Congress. The room's focal point is a stained glass window showing George Washington kneeling in prayer. Behind him is etched these words from psalm 16:1: "Preserve me. O God. for in thee do I put my trust."

The Supreme Court.

Above the head of the Chief Justice of the Supreme Court are the Ten Commandments, with the great American eagle protecting them. Moses is included among the great lawgivers in Herman A. MacNeil's marble sculpture group on the east front. The crier who opens each session closes with the words, "God save the United States and the Honorable Court."

The Washington Monument.

Engraved on the metal cap on the top of the Washington Monument are the words: "Praise be to God." Lining the walls of the stairwell are such biblical phrases as "Search the Scriptures," "Holiness to the Lord," "Train up a child in the way he should go, and when he is old he will not depart from it."

Lincoln Memorial.

Millions have stood in the Lincoln Memorial and gazed up at the statue of the great Abraham Lincoln. The sculptor who chiseled the features of Lincoln in granite all but seems to make Lincoln speak his own words inscribed into the walls.

"...That this Nation, under God, shall have a new birth of freedom, and that government of the people, by the people, for the people, shall not perish from the earth."

At the opposite end, on the north wall, his Second Inaugural Address alludes to "God," the "Bible," "providence," "the Almighty," and "divine attributes."

It then continues:

"As was said 3000 years ago, so it still must be said, 'The judgments of the Lord are true and righteous altogether.'"

The Library Of Congress.

Numerous quotations from Scripture can be found within its walls. One reminds each American of his responsibility to his Maker: "What doth the Lord require of thee, but to do justly and love mercy and walk humbly with thy God" (Micah 6:8)

Another in the lawmaker's library preserves the Psalmist's acknowledgment that all nature reflects the order and beauty of the Creator. "The heavens declare the glory of God, and the firmament showeth His handiwork" (Psalm 19:1).

And still another reference: "The light shineth in darkness, and the darkness comprehendeth it not" (John 1:5).

From *The Rebirth of America*
Printed by permission by Arthur S. DeMoss Foundation

56

From *The Rebirth of America*

When in Washington I love gazing upon the scriptures and Christian sayings. Is everything bearing the name of God going to be sandblasted? How long will the money say IN GOD WE TRUST? When the money is replaced by the SMART CARD do you think God will get His due?

I want a President to stand up and say "This country was founded on Godly principles and that is the way it will remain". You are a people pleaser; you could win over millions of Americans if you announced the rights for Christians, tell America and the ACLU to stop the persecution. Tell us that we can have prayer at football games the way we used to, tell us we can pray and mention the name of God at school graduations, tell us our children can write stories about God if they want to and not get punished for it, tell us we can celebrate Christmas and the birth of Jesus publicly, tell us we can talk about our faith in the work place and not get fired.

"Congress shall make no law respecting an establishment of religion, or prohibiting the free exercise thereof; or abridging the freedom of speech, or of the press, or the right of the people peaceably to assemble, and to petition the Government for a redress of grievances."

U.S. Constitution, First Amendment

Christians are clearly fair game for ridicule; much of the media portrays churches and pastors in a very negative light. Christians founded this country, they have always been here. Did you ever see the movie "Invasion of the Body Snatchers"? Somehow that movie reminds me of the threat Christians will be facing if the persecution is not stopped. Things never remain the same, they are always in the process of getting better or worse.

Before I stray too far from the classroom, I want to talk to you about OUTCOME BASED EDUCATION. This "educational reform" will force our children to learn "correct" opinions. This sounds like brainwashing to me. There is already a test that has been prepared and given in some places that will evaluate the childs "political correctness". If the child believes in God or comes from a home where Christian values are practiced, there is special orientation that child will receive until their thinking lines up with the humanistic agenda. This is dehumanizing and frightening!

OBE teaches that there are no absolutes, no right or wrong. Education becomes consensus not truth. Instead of teaching information such as reading, writing, mathematics, history, etc., feelings and attitudes are emphasized. Morals and anything of a religious nature are rejected. And then we have the nerve to ask what has happened to our children.

Martin Luther King, Jr. was quoted as saying "Communism is based on ethical relativism and accepts no stable moral absolutes. Right and wrong are related to the most expedient methods for dealing with class war.

I am much afraid that schools will prove to be great gates of hell unless they diligently labor in explaining the holy scriptures, engraving them in the hearts of youth. I advise no one to place his child where the scriptures do not reign paramount. Every institution in which men are not increasingly occupied with the Word of God must become corrupt.

Martin Luther King

Communism exploits the dreadful philosophy that the end justifies the means. It enunciates movingly the theory of a classless society, but alas!, its methodologies for achieving this noble end are all too often ignoble."

KEEP THIS IN MIND

The following excerpt from a file on `Communist Rules for Revolution' was obtained by the Armed Forces in Dusseldorf in May, 1919. It might explain some of today's happenings.

A. Corrupt the young; get them away from religion. Get them interested in sex. Make them superficial; destroy their ruggedness.
B. Get control of all means of publicity and thereby:

1. Get people's minds off their government by focusing their attention on athletics, sexy books and plays and other trivialities.
2. Divide the people into hostile groups by constantly harping on controversial matters of no importance.
3. Destroy the people's faith in their natural leaders by holding the latter up to contempt, ridicule, and obloguy.
4. Always preach true democracy but seize power as fast and as ruthlessly as possible.
5. By encouraging government extravagances, destroy its credit, produce fear of inflation with rising prices and generous discount.
6. Ferment unnecessary strikes in vital industries, encourage civil disorders, and foster a lenient and soft attitude on the part of government toward such disorders.
7. By specious argument cause the breakdown of the old moral virtues, honesty, sobriety, continence, faith in the pledged word and ruggedness.
8. Cause the registration of all firearms on some pretext with the view of confiscation of them and leaving the population helpless.

Does there seem to be a parallel of thought in the present day trend of events?

The text books are even more scaring. History has been completely rewritten. What is wrong with the true history of this country? Children need to know their heritage. Emotional growth is healthier knowing where we came from. Look at men and women who search for their biological parents, their need is built in to know their roots. The same for us all , we function as a body and knowing our past helps us to understand our future.

The great men of history who paved the way are being eliminated; George Washington is barely touched on. One of the saddest changes is the story of the Pilgrims and Thanksgiving; we were always taught they gave thanks to God. God is no longer mentioned, now it has the Pilgrims giving thanks to the Indians. The new books are also painting a negative picture of America. Is this to prepare their formable minds for ONE WORLD < SOCIALISTIC thinking?

Is it any wonder many children are confused and are living without hope for the future. Think about this! Children no longer are taught to be patriotic, so there is no love of country, children no longer have respect for parents and teachers. Children no longer value life because abortion is not even questioned among the young and because of the "death" education that small children have been put through. Children no longer have heroes because we destroy our own. Almost every politician and celebrity that has passed on has been defamed. Children no longer can talk about God freely with friends in school, teachers punish little children for doing so or for trying to tell others to meet them at the flagpole for prayer.

"A nation which does not remember what it was yesterday, does not know what it is today, nor what it is trying to do. We are trying to do a futile thing if we do not know where we came from or what we have been about.

Woodrow Wilson

Many children have been stripped of all that's good. Children used to laugh and have fun, play games, they were innocent. No more. When you see a child you can see the emptiness in their eyes, they just go through the motions. And then we ask why the drugs, sex, suicide's. My heart breaks for our youth.

If you're not familiar with the "death" education I mentioned it goes something like this — — — there is a row boat and in it are your Mommy, Daddy, Sister, Brother and your best friend, the boat is too heavy so one person must be eliminated, which one would you throw overboard and let drown? This is sick and emotionally damaging. This is just one of the games that have been introduced into the schools.

Lately it has been discovered that there are sex games going on in the name of education. Children are being shown sex films on homosexuality, actual sex acts including bestiality. These particular situations may not be school policy, however, the individual teacher takes it upon him or herself to implement these programs. There are so many things going on in the schools that would disgust you. Most parents are not aware of what is going on, however, the ones that are, are starting to fight back.

Mr. President there is so much I am getting off my chest. This is just a sampling of what is taking place out there. I could write volumes, I won't. Isn't it interesting that in any organization or institution that one can mention, one can find injustice connected to it? Everything that comes to mind has been turned topsy-turvey and not at all what it started out to be, including our Constitution.

I realize you are not responsible for all the ills of the country, it started long before you were born. My Grandmother said it would sneak up on us, and sure enough the time is here. The concern of many of your critics is, it appears, you are going along with the destruction of everything our forefathers held dear more than any President we have had.

Of course, any leader is bait to be pulled, prodded, bribed, coerced and even threatened by those around him, by special interest-groups and the "powers that be." The difference is a true "statesman" WILL NOT be swayed! A man of principles WILL NOT be swayed! A man of integrity WILL NOT be swayed! A committed man of God who has a personal relationship with his Lord WILL NOT be swayed, he is unshakable, unmovable and stands on God's word at every turn for every decision.

The men of yesteryear were wise beyond measure. The words of wisdom you are about to read came from John Smalley, a 1756 Yale graduate. He held a pastorate for fifty years at Farmington (New Britain), Connecticut. This is a small part of a sermon Smalley preached on May 8, 1800, about the evils of government.

Let not good Men despond: not let them relax their exertions to repel, as long and as extensively as they can, the prevalence of error, irreligion and wretchedness. Mightier is he that is with them, than all that are against them. When it is asked in the eleventh psalm: "If the foundations be destroyed, what can the righteous do?" the answer is short, but very emphatical and abundantly sufficient: "The Lord is in his holy temple; the Lord's throne is in heaven. Elsewhere, the psalmist, adoring the power and wisdom of the most High, says, "Surely the wrath of man shall praise thee; the remainder of the wrath shalt thou restrain." It is often said, "Christ is able to Support his Own church and minister, without the aid of human laws." This is doubtless true, it is also true, that Christ is able to take care of his Church, and to bring the many sons given him to glory, without any ministers at all. And equally true is it that God is able to govern the nations, without the help of earthly rulers. But, from the e premises, the consequence will not follow, without hard drawing, that men may innocently and safely neglect exerting the power they have, for the support, either of good government, or of uncorrupted Christianity. "Those that walk in pride, God is able to abase"; but is there therefore nothing hazardous, nor wrong, in thus walking? A curse was once denounced, on them who "came not to the help of the Lord, against the mighty["]; though the Lord helped himself, without their assistance. But the foregoing truths, however they may have been perverted to the countenancing of human negligence in the cause of God or

Christ, are matter of just consolation to the pious and good, when they walk in darkness and have no light: when they see little probability that their utmost efforts for the support of order, or of undefiled religion, will have any effect.

There will always be some, and some that ought to be leaders and teachers, whose policy it is, to turn with the times; to swim with the tide, and swing with the vibrating pendulum of popular opinion. Who will trim their way to seek love; and "become all things to all if by all means they may save" themselves. But a steadfast adherence to truth and duty, however great the apparent danger, is the only way of real safety. He who thus "loses his life, shall save it": and he shall lose his life who would save it, by deserting his post or hiding himself under refuges of falsehood, when evil is foreseen "The fearful and unbelieving, shall have their part" at last, in the same lake with bolder transgressors. "The fear of man bringeth a snare; but whoso putteth his trust in the Lord shall be safe." For the encouragement of good men, in perilous times, and particularly of good rulers, it is written: "He that walketh righteously, and speaketh uprightly; he that despiseth the gain of oppressions, that shaketh his hands from holding of bribes, that stoppeth his ears from hearing of blood, and shutteth his eyes from seeing evil; he shall dwell on high; his place of defence shall be the munitions of rocks: bread shall be, given him, his waters shall be sure." On these grounds is the exhortation in Isaiah, a few chapters after our text, with which I shall conclude. "Say ye not, A confederacy, to all them to whom this people shall say, A confederacy: neither fear ye their fear, nor be afraid Sanctify the Lord of hosts himself; and let him be your fear, and let Him be your dread."

Printed from "Political Sermons of the American Founding Era"

1730 - 1805

Ellis Sandoz - Liberty Fund Inc. Indianapolis, Indiana

Being a people pleaser, you are naturally eager to please everybody, it doesn't work that way. Stand for what you believe! If you don't, it will be your downfall, politically and personally. You may think you have protection and favor now, however, what happens when you are no longer of use, when you have completed the work that you were put in there to do?

When one becomes too familiar with anything, it loses it's punch. This next scripture has been freely bandied about, therefore, let us all read it together slowly, several times.

> *If my people which, are called by my name, shall humble themselves, and pray, and seek my face, and turn from their wicked ways; then will I hear from Heaven, and will forgive their sin, and will heal their land.*

> II Chronicles 7:14

In your acceptance speech you said "THE PEOPLE RULE", I don't think so. Washington is telling the people what is good for them without asking the people what they want. People are screaming LESS GOVERNMENT!! STOP REGULATING OUR LIVES FROM WASHINGTON!! Stop and think about it, who gave the government the right to tell us what to do in every area of our lives, we were a free people! We can no longer have our own opinions without consequences, unless of course that opinion is politically correct..

Sometimes the thought of the Old West sure appeals to my baser instincts. Claim some land, build a house with some help from a neighbor, who helps just for the sake of helping. The good part is I can rent to whom I want and I can even knock out a wall without a permit from the city. When I want to go to town, I won't have to worry about change for the parking meter.

The fact that people have actually gotten arrested for putting money in a strangers parking meter so they would not get a ticket, shows us the insanity of our times. It's that reversal thing about good now being seen as evil.

Prayer by Dr. Bill Bright

... to open a joint session of the Florida Legislature, March 5, 1997

*Dr. Bill Bright is President of Campus Crusade for Christ International. By invitation Dr. Bright prayed the prayer which follows. **A storm of protest broke out upon its conclusion.** Let us pray it in agreement, and also ask God to give us more principled leaders like Dr. and Mrs. Bright.*

Holy Father, Almighty God, Creator of the Universe of more than a hundred billion galaxies, we bow in reverence and awe before you. You are holy and righteous, loving and forgiving, you are faithful and just. There is no one like you; you alone are worthy of our trust and praise. In this day of relativism and political correctness, we've abandoned our absolutes. As a result, our nation is in danger losing its soul. We've become a morally and spiritually bankrupt society; we have discarded your time-honored Ten Commandments and no longer practice the Golden Rule. We have insulted you, the God of our founding fathers, and turned to our own selfish materialistic pursuits.

*The false gods of gold and entertainment have captured our minds and hearts. You have both encouraged us and warned us in your Holy Word, the bible, which has been outlawed from our schools, that if we obey your laws, you will bless many nations. **For the first 170 years of our history, you blessed us beyond any nation in all of history, because of our godly forefathers. Yet, you have also warned us that if we violate your laws and turn away from your love and protection, you will remove your blessings and we shall reap the bitter fruit of our selfish, sinful deeds.** History is replete with examples of those nations which have denied you and served the gods of gold and power. Germany, Russia, North Korea, Cuba are several current illustrations of what happens to nations who turn their backs on you. Now our own beloved country is rapidly becoming another example of what happens when we no longer are protected by your grace.*

***The answer to all of our personal and national problems is so obvious. If only we obeyed your Ten Commandments and the Golden Rule, as a people, all our problems would be solved.** Father you've commanded us to pray for our leaders, for all those in authority over us. We are fully aware that our leaders from the precinct to the White House set the standards for the rest of the nation. Therefore, I hold before you these men and women whom you have honored and placed in leadership over us. I pray for them individually and as a body, that they will seek your guidance and your wisdom, that they will use their gifts and influence to help restore us to our former allegiances and trust in you. That they, their families, and associates will experience your special blessings.*

*We remember the promise which you gave to King Solomon for ancient Israel, as recorded in Chronicles, chapter 7, verse 14, **"If my people, who are called by my name, will humble themselves and pray and seek my face and turn from their wicked ways, then will I hear from heaven, forgive their sins, and heal their land."** We claim this promise for Florida and for America, that once again we may be a nation under your sovereign holy, righteous, and loving rule. Thank you, Father, for this great country where we still enjoy the freedom to seek after you in different ways through various religions, which I respect and defend. I come to you, Father, in the name of the one whom you sent to be my savior, whom I love more than my own life - the Lord Jesus Christ. We worship you and we praise you, and adore you, the true God, the only God. May blessing be upon this group of men and women in an unprecedented way. For the good of our country and for the glory and praise of your incomparable name. Amen!*

—from P & R Schenck, Associates in Evangelism, 601 Pennsylvania Ave., N. W., Suite 900, Washington, D.C. 20004.

The legitimate purpose of government since the founding of America has been to protect the lives, liberty, and property of its citizens. James Madison summed it up well when he said, "We have staked the whole future of American civilization, not upon the power of government, far from it. We have staked the future of all our political institutions upon the capacity of each and all of us to govern ourselves, to control ourselves, to sustain ourselves according to the Ten Commandments of God".

Our founding fathers based our system of government on the First Commandment, **"Thou shalt have no other gods before me"**. They understood that man was created to serve God, not the state. They implemented a system with clear limits upon what government could and could not do. This was with scrutiny, carefully carried out to ensure individual freedom.

The framers of our Constitution made it very clear that the people were to govern themselves under God's laws. Government should never have the power to deprive individuals of rights that the Constitution stated were "endowed by their Creator". The Declaration of Independence states that governments derive "their just Powers from the Consent of the Governed," and that "whenever any Form of Government becomes destructive of these Ends, it is the Right of the People to alter or to abolish it".

Mr. President, do you understand why more and more citizens are angry and disillusioned? Not only because our basic freedoms are threatened but because people are working harder and earning less. The government now takes more than 40% of income earned compared to 3% in 1928. If it continues at the same rate we will all (except the elite) be working for the state and waiting in bread lines.

Instead of trusting in the government primarily as a source of protection from foreign or domestic enemies, Americans have embraced the very centralized government the founding fathers urged them to fear. The economic controls that have proliferated in the United States in recent decades have not only restricted our freedom to use our economic resources, but they have also affected our freedom of speech, of press and of religion. We have been educated towards dependency rather than liberty; we have been brainwashed by television and books to believe that it is the responsibility of government to take resources from some and bestow them upon others.

Why has this happened? Because men are playing God. When you have men who do not understand what it means to let God reign, we will have tyranny and abuse.

Over the past forty years, as government has become evermore dominant in our lives, and as government programs were established to help our people, instead, it has changed the way we behave, corrupted our values and diminished our virtue. We have looked more and more towards Caesar to take care of us and to protect us in what Margaret Thatcher called the "nanny state." We have increasingly turned away from family and faith. In rendering unto Caesar, we have stopped rendering unto God.

Our now "value-free" government rewards us when we fail and taxes us when we succeed. Inheritance taxes force families to sell off farms and businesses every day in America as the lifework of our families goes to the government and not to our children. The saddest of all is the husband and wife who work hard all their lives and when they retire cannot afford to keep their home because of taxes. In plain English, it can be said the government takes homes away from old people, and these are the same people who helped support the government all their working years.

The answers to the countries ills are basically simple and many an average citizen could give you the answers. However, for reasons unexplained to the American public the obvious and common sense approach is side stepped. Let's try to make it easier for people to obey the simple rules, to do justice, to love mercy and to walk humbly with God. Removing the corrosive influence of government will make a revival of American values possible.

Thinking back on when so many changes started to take place, I find the social disintegration took a turn about 1961. Presidents and congressional leaders have, during the last three decades, given America an echo, not a choice by proposing and supporting budgets and programs that smack of neo-Marxism.

During the last thirty-five years, Democrats and Republicans alike have supported a massive expansion in what the federal government does and how much it costs. The federal tax take has increased from $94 billion in 1961 to some $1.4 trillion in 1997. Spending has grown even more - from less than $100 billion in 1961 to more than $1.6 trillion per year. Interest on the national debt went from $9 billion in 1961 to $345 billion of our tax dollars in 1997.

Now I ask you honestly, is America better off because of these programs that never existed prior to the 1960's? The Department of Education, the Department of Housing and Urban Development, the National Endowment for the Arts, the Legal Services Corp., food stamps, billions of dollars in subsidies to Planned Parenthood, Gay Men's Health Crisis, etc. These are the same organizations calling the Christian dangerous and are directly going against the word of God. And my own government has put them in place, defends their actions and promotes them as being a good thing. As most things go, I'm sure they were well-meaning at the start.

As long as our federal government moves unabated into the areas of welfare, education, crime, civil rights, and health care, the power-grab will continue. It seems everyday there is another new law, guideline, executive order, ruling, decision,

68

regulation or ordinance whose result is an unconstitutional intrusion on our ever-weakening rights as Americans — making government stronger and families weaker. Government was originally set up to be a servant of the people, not our lord and master.

The proper role for civil government is to safeguard our God-given rights to life, liberty and property. The federal government has those powers which were delegated to it by the states or provided by amendment, and which specifically are enumerated in the Constitution. IT HAS NO OTHER LICIT AUTHORITY.

America grew to greatness because there was no doubt about the source of authority. God Almighty was acknowledged to be Saviour, sovereign and lawgiver. As of late God's law originating with the Bible and incorporated in the common law, can be readily overturned subject to whim and mandated by "political correctness." America's common-law heritage keeps us under the laws of God, but the new world order is changing that rapidly.

It is difficult to go back from whence we came, however, if we don't begin to respect Gods Law, America will self-destruct. Mr. President, you are a smart man, some say brilliant, but what about common sense. Common sense tells us IT AIN'T WORKING! The average age of the worlds great civilizations has been 200 years. These nations progressed through this sequence:

From Bondage to Spiritual Faith
From Spiritual Faith to Great Courage
From Courage to Liberty
From Liberty to Abundance
From Abundance to Selfishness
From Selfishness to Complacency
From Complacency to Apathy
From Apathy to Dependency
From Dependency Back Again into Bondage

Recently, I met Alexy Steele, a young Russian artist who echoes my thoughts exactly. He spoke with more passion than most Americans, about what has happened to this country and why. He could give the Senate and Congress an earful. He talked of our culture and how the obvious counterculture is working fervently against everything our Western civilization has stood for. In his own words, "If it keeps going this way America is doomed, you are at a serious crossroads, in a few years it will be too late. The government must get deep down to the core of the issues and stop getting stuck on the words, mutual ground is a necessity, you must reestablish the principles of the Western civilization as they were. The entire game must be destroyed and a totally new pattern of thinking needs to replace the thinking that got America in this mess. Change the rules of the game! This concerns everyone, it must be a nonpartisan way of doing things". Alexy continued, "Man is not ready for the advances of the technology for the 21st Century. What you have been doing does not work!"

Coming from Russia he saw how the things that are going on here were at one time a part of his country and he compared how it didn't work in Russia either. He is more aware than most Americans what trouble these United States are in.

Alexy explained, " Art is the reflection of the inner man of this world — music, art, film and TV are a clear reflection of the condition of our society". Before you read farther reread that statement. That is a mouth full!

Think about it! The entertainment we watch, the books we read, they are a reflection of the inner man who produces it. Where God is void in the inner man you see darkness, perverseness, violence, etc.. Where God is present you find light, goodness and positive influences for the society as a whole.

With each new dilemma there is a new bill written up and passed to rectify the problem. We should know by now that passing laws does not take care of the human heart. Getting back to basics and relying on the original instruction manual is the only answer. The handbook (Bible) for living are God's laws that change for the better. As my conversation with Alexy was coming to a close, he left me with this profound statement, "The ability to believe (in God) separates man from the beast".

It is the beast that causes man to sin. Many people have a hard time with that word sin. However, it is what it is, sin is simply rebelling against God and can come in several forms. We all have sinned and come short of the glory of God. Sins can be very subtle, let us all take inventory:

Subtle Sins

Addiction	Factions	Lukewarmness
Anger	Fear	Lying
Animosity	Gluttony	Materialism
Anxiety	Gossip Indulgence	Negativism
Bitterness	Guilt	Prayerlessness
Boastfulness	Half-Truths	Prejudice
Closed Mindedness	Hatred	Pride
Condemnation	Haughtiness	Purposelessness
Condescension	Hostility	Rebellion
Covetousness	Idolatry	Resentment
Critical Nature	Immoral Fantasies	Rudeness
Deception	Impatience	Self-Righteousness
Demanding	Impurity	Selfish Ambition
Depression	Indifference	Selfishness
Discord	Inflexibility	Skepticism
Discouragement	Insincerity	Temperamental
Dissension	Intemperance	Unbelief or Lack of Faith
Dogmatism	Irritability	Unforgiveness
Domination	Jealousy	Ungratefulness
Egoism	Judgment	Vanity
Emotional Abuse	Lack of Affection	
Envy	Laziness	

"If we confess our sins, He is faithful and just to forgive us our sins and to cleanse us from from all unrighteousness." I John 1-9

Subtle Sins from "Discipled Foundation Plan", published by Amy Foundation, Lansing, Michigan.

President Clinton, here are some of your own words quoted in U.S. News & World Report, April 4, 1994. President Clinton says he considers himself a person who has "sinned as a child of God, who has sought forgiveness, searched for redemption and is struggling to grow and to find the guidance of God in this job. I do not believe I could do my job as President, much less continue to grow as a person, in the absence of my faith in God."

I loved reading that, however, this confuses the Christian community. As I mentioned earlier your politics among other actions do not appear to line up Biblically. You say you are a believer, and I believe you are, then why and how are decisions made that go directly against the very clear Word of the living God? Going to church is wonderful, reading your Bible is wonderful, claiming you are a Christian is wonderful, however, your decisions are slapping God right in the face. President Clinton, we see you carrying your Bible, please take a stand for it.[6]

Going to church doesn't make you a Christian anymore than going to a garage makes you an automobile.

W.A. "Billy" Sunday

[6] The Sins of Compromise — Page 137

72

For those that do not share the Judeo-Christian perspective, I'm sorry. God will deal with them in His way in His time. Their anger and disapproval should not, must not, be a consideration. If they knew the reality of the separation from God in the life hereafter they would believe real quick. However, those rejecting God have free will to do so. No one is pushing a belief down their throats, yet they should not be catered to for fear of offending them by talking about the God of the universe. That is insanity!! Some people like peanut butter, some don't. We still have peanut butter on the shelves in every supermarket to see. The millions who do believe in God do not have legitimate reason, responsibility or duty whatsoever to dismantle our entire public affirmation of faith in God just to please a minority who do not believe in anything.

I spoke to soon! I just heard on the news an activist group concerned about people with allergies to peanuts want to ban peanut butter and jelly sandwiches from schools. They also are proposing to set aside three rows of seats in airplanes to be a designated "peanut free zone".

God's hand has been removed to a large degree as Americans run amuck. We are still under a certain amount of grace. However, how long do we expect God to be patient with a country He blessed, prospered, gave complete freedom to worship Him and His Son and we now have the nerve to ignore, wipe out and act ashamed to say His name? **America is shaking her fist in the face of a holy God and she will not get away with it.**[7]

Remember therefore from whence thou art fallen, and repent, and do the first works; or else I will remove thy candlestick (lampstand) out of his place, except thou repent.

Revelation 2:5

---

[7] The lampstand: Is It Leaving America — Page 143

God breathed life into you and me, He hung the moon and stars, He is the Alpha and Omega, the beginning and the end. We are His children and we are to obey. If we go against His will we will pay, especially when we know right from wrong and are choosing the wrong. No one gets out of this life without paying the price, not even the President of the United States.

We all pay for our actions at some point, "We reap what we sow" are not just words. If for some reason you are in a place where you cannot do the right thing, then you do not belong there. You have the power to make or break, to build up or destroy a nation, in fact the world. You and God together can move mountains for this nation. You can be a miracle-working President going down in history like no other, but not on your own strength. Surrender to God's will. Surrendering the ego is tough for power-driven intellectuals. However, surrendering it is one of the main keys to the Kingdom. Surrender! Give it all to God.

God knows our hearts. We can fool others but we never fool God. God has the solution to everything, whatever the problem, the answer is always the same (surrender). We are amiss when we say we have given Him the problem and we still continue to figure out the solution. When we give something to God that is exactly what we need to do — GIVE IT TO HIM and then forget it (release it).

Whosever therefore shall confess me before men, him will I confess also before my Father which is in heaven. But whosever shall deny me before men, him will I also deny before my Father which is in heaven.

Matthew 10:32,33

Be not deceived; God is not mocked: for whatsoever a man soweth, that shall he also reap. For he that soweth to his flesh shall of the flesh reap corruption; but he that soweth to the spirit shall of the spirit reap life everlasting.

Galatians 6:7&8

God ONLY fixes it when we do not take it back and stress or worry over it. God moves for those who believe Him, and totally depend on Him. He will not move for those who think they can work it out for themselves. When I learned that lesson, it simplified my life and I've never been the same.

And yes, God did give us a brain and free will to do as we please, however, when we do as we please look at how we mess up our lives. When we follow His rules and let Jesus be the Lord of our life, LIFE WORKS. Through the Father (God), the Son (Jesus), and the Holy Spirit (Comforter) who takes up residence in us, we are given joy, peace, love, and a life of blessings.

You say you are a servant to the people. Your first servanthood is to your Lord, then the people. Being one of the most powerful men in the world is an awesome responsibility, as you must be aware of every day. I'm asking you to think about it in a new light, think of Jesus watching your every move. In every decision say to yourself, "WHAT WOULD JESUS DO?" Will God be able to say, " Well done good and faithful servant"?

PRESIDENT WILLIAM JEFFERSON CLINTON, THESE ARE YOUR WORDS THAT CAME OUT OF YOUR MOUTH AT THE DEMOCRATIC CONVENTION IN ATLANTA, AUGUST OF 1992!

> *"We have seen the folks in Washington turn the American ethic on its head. For too long, those who play by the rules and keep the faith have gotten the shaft. And those who cut corners and cut deals have been rewarded."*
>
> Bill Clinton

THINK ABOUT WHERE YOU WERE AND WHAT YOU WERE SAYING IN AUGUST OF 1998!

From the desk of Rev. Lorraine D. Coconato:

To: April Shenendoah

Dear April:
    When the Lord woke me to receive this "word," after He delivered it, He told me to send a letter and a copy of it to the President, since this was a "word" to the Church and President Clinton is a professing believer.

    When I gave it to Pastor Scott Bauer, he loved it but he thought that President Clinton would not heed 't.

    I read in Time magazine this morning that Rev. Jerry Falwell was prompted to send a similar letter!

    Call me if you have any questions or comments. I will probably be out until 1:30 p.m.

Love in Christ,

Lorraine

Leaves of Healing Ministries
19719 Crystal Hills Drive
Northridge, Ca. 91326

President Bill Clinton   Mar. 17, 1998
The White House
Washington, D. C.

Dear Mr. President:

I am an evangelist/pastor in a local church in the Los Angeles area. During the night, I was awakened with this word from the Lord. He directed me to send you a copy of this message, as well as this accompanying exhortation.

Mr. President, as you have professed your faith in the Lord Jesus Christ, you are not only a divinely appointed leader for this nation, but a brother in the faith. I honor you in the position that God has placed you in and I regularly pray for you and your administration that you would make wise decisions that are pleasing to the Lord.

Mr. President, in light of all the media attention regarding the alleged indiscretions in your life, I need to encourage you to hear the Word of the Lord in 2 Timothy 2: 19, "Nevertheless the solid foundation of God stands, having this seal: 'The Lord knows those who are His,' and 'Let

2

everyone who names the name of Christ depart from iniquity." The scripture also tells us in Luke 14:11, "For whoever exalts himself will be humbled and he who humbles himself will be exalted."

Mr. President, I do not judge or condemn you for the things that you may have done. For, I, myself, am a sinner, who is saved by His grace.

In God's Word, Mr. President, there were many kings and rulers who repented before God for their personal transgressions, as well as the iniquity of the nation. The king and ruler that humbles himself before God and submits to the ways of the Lord, will be exalted. He who continues in his sin and rebels against the ways of the Lord, will be afflicted.

Mr. President, God's heart is to bless you and this nation! I admonish you in the name of the Lord, as a minister of the gospel of Jesus Christ, to repent of any wrongdoing or immorality before God, to your wife and daughter and before the nation! You are not required to give details of your transgression to the nation, but you are required to confess your sins to the Lord and as 1 John 1:9 says, "He is faithful and just to forgive us our sins and cleanse us from all unrighteousness."

3

The United States is a great and mighty nation. abundantly blessed of God. Mr. President, will you prayerfully consider this petition?

My prayers are with you, Mr. President, Mrs. Clinton, your family and the nation. As the minister of the national government and as an ambassador to the nations of the world, please consider these words!

In Service and Reverence to His Name,

Rev. Lorraine D. Coconato

Rev. Lorraine D. Coconato

Prophecy received by Rev. Lorraine D. Coconato.

2:20 a.m.- Mar. 17, 1998

I will sweep through My church and clean the debris,
Ministries will rise and ministries will fall.

I will work mighty signs, wonders and miracles in your midst,
To declare My glory, to define My love for My people.

For I have given you an everlasting covenant and My Word I will not revoke!
My Spirit will cleanse, purify and refine.
My heart is to bless yet will I judge those who transgress My Words.

For, I, the Lord, am rich in mercy and grace and I will visit you with multiple visits in these days,
For that which I have spoken, I will perform and that which is broken, I will restore.

Speak forth My truth; preach the truth, live truth and reveal truth. For I am Truth and My truth will set you free, says the Lord.

We all want *truth*, or so I would like to believe. What we as individuals believe, is our own *truth*. However, what about God's *truth*? President Clinton, in your speech at the National Prayer Breakfast, you said … "I say to you, we will always have our differences, we will never know the whole *truth*." Mr. President, I say to you that we can absolutely know *truth* through the sword of the spirit, which is the Bible and the living Word of the living God.

The book of Jude, located directly before Revelations, speaks of God's *truth*. Jude wrote in verses 1-16 about motivating Christians everywhere to action. He wanted them to recognize the dangers of false teaching, to protect themselves and other believers, and to win back those who had already been deceived. Jude was writing against godless teachers who were saying that Christians could do as they pleased without fear of God's punishment. Jude's letter warns against living a nominal Christian life and tells us it is our duty to fight for God's *truth*. Read verses 17-23 below, and determine to stand firm defending God's *truth* at all costs.

---

[17]But, dear friends, remember what the apostles of our Lord Jesus Christ foretold. [18]They said to you, "In the last times there will be scoffers who will follow their own ungodly desires." [19]These are the men who divide you, who follow mere natural instincts and do not have the spirit. [20]But you, dear friends, build yourselves up in your most holy faith and pray in the Holy Spirit. [21]Keep yourselves in God's love as you wait for the mercy of our Lord Jesus Christ to bring you to eternal life. [22]Be Merciful to those who doubt; [23]snatch others from the fire and save them; to others show mercy, mixed with fear – **hating even the clothing stained by corrupted flesh.**

EXCERPTS FROM REMARKS BY
PRESIDENT
BILL CLINTON

First…this prayer breakfast is an important time to reaffirm that in this nation where we have freedom of religion, we need not seek freedom from religion.

I am honored that all of you are here, not for a political purpose…We come here to seek the help and guidance of our Lord, putting aside our differences as men and women who freely acknowledge that we can't have all the answers. And we come here seeking to restore, renew, and strengthen our faith…The Scriptures tell us we need faith as a source of strength, the assurance of things hoped for, and the conviction of things unseen.

What it means to me is that here, if we have enough faith, in spite of all the pressures to the contrary, we can define ourselves from the inside out, in a town where everybody tries to define you from the outside in.

We need our faith as a source of hope. Faith teaches us that each of us is capable of redemption and, therefore, that progress is possible. Not perfection, but progress.

We need our faith as a source of challenge. If we read the Scriptures carefully, it teaches us that all of us must strive to live by what we believe or, in more conventional terms, to live out the admonition of President Kennedy that here on earth, God's work must truly be our own.

But, perhaps most important of all for me, we need our faith, each of us—president, vice president, senator, congressman, general, justice—as a source of humility and to remind us that we are all sinners. St. Paul once said, "The very thing which I would not do, and that which I would, that I do not." And even more, not only because we do wrong, but because we don't always know what is right.

…I say to you, we will always have our differences, we will never know the whole truth, of course that this true. But hopefully we have learned today again that we must seek to know the will of God and live by it, that to do it we have to give up our bitterness and resentment, that we have to learn to forgive ourselves and one another and that we have to fight, as hard as it is, to be honest and fair…

I have always been touched by the living example of Jesus Christ. All the religious leaders of his day were suspicious of him and always tried to trap him because he was so at ease with the hurting, the hungry, the lonely and, yes, the sinners. In one of the attempts to trick Christ, he was asked what is the greatest commandment. And he answered, quoting Moses, "You shall love the Lord your God with all your heart and with all your soul and with all your mind." And then he added, as we should add, "this is the great and foremost commandment, and the second is like it, you shall love your neighbor as yourself."

Re pent (ri pent), *v. i.* feel sorry for having done wrong and seek forgiveness: *The sinner repented.* —*v. t.* feel sorry for; regret: *repent one's choice.* [<Old French *repentir*, ultimately <Latin *re-* repeatedly + *paenitere* cause to regret] — re pent er, *n.*

ISAIAH SPEAKS

God offers mercy to America ...and to us all. In spite of the hardened, idolatrous ways of His people, God revealed Himself not only as a just and vengeful God, but also as a merciful, long suffering God of covenant love. With eyes of faith, Isaiah saw a Saviour who would one day take on Himself the full fury and wrath of a holy God against sin.

Mercy was abundant then and is still available today, if God's people will only meet His conditions.

1.   Return to God's Word. "Hear the Word of the Lord...give ear unto the law of our God" (Isaiah 1:10).
2.   Repent. "Wash you, make you clean: put away the evil of your doings from before my eyes; cease to do evil" (Isaiah 1:1).
3.   Restore God as King and His righteousness as the standard for living. "Come ye, and let us walk in the light of the Lord... Learn to do well; seek judgement, relieve the oppressed... If ye be willing and obedient, ye shall eat the good of the land" (Isaiah 2:5; 1:7,19).

When we are removing all that is good from our society and replacing it with evil, what can we expect but a country falling apart at the seams. You talk of REPAIRING THE BREACH, with all due respect Mr. President, man dresses the wound, God heals it. If you are not REPAIRING THE BREACH with God's help or with His Book of instructions, then all the dialogue will be empty words, and the actions futile. Well meaning with no substance. The stripping of God from government and the American people automatically equals a corrupt nation.

> *Wherefore thus saith the Holy One of Israel, Because ye despise this word, and trust in oppression and perverseness, and stay thereon:*
>
> *Therefore this iniquity shall be to you as a BREACH ready to fall, swelling out in a high wall, whose breaking cometh suddenly at an instant.*

ISAIAH 30: 12,13

President Clinton, God says in His Word He will spew lukewarm Christians out of His mouth (Revelations 3:16). I implore you to take a stand for your Lord. Do not be concerned about doing the popular thing in man's eyes, be concerned about the consequences if you do not do the righteous thing in God's eyes. He is the rewarder of our faith. If you are a "born again" blood bought man of God, then you can claim Isaiah 58:12, the same scripture you laid your hand on, in the Holy Bible, as you were being sworn in for your second term as President.

> *And they that shall be of thee shall build the old waste places: thou shalt raise up the foundations of many generations; and thou shalt be called, The REPAIRER OF THE BREACH The restorer of paths to dwell in.*

Isaiah 58:12

President Clinton, many times throughout this letter I wanted to call you Bill, however, because I respect the office you hold I refrained from doing so. Please allow me this one time.

Bill, dear child of God, the all knowing, all powerful, sovereign Ruler of the universe is eagerly waiting to manifest Himself to you, to our nation, and to a generation that has never clearly known God. Mr. President the hour is late. God's judgement has rapidly begun to fall. Perhaps like Sodom and Gomorrah, God would be willing to spare our nation if just a few righteous could be found. Could it be as in the days of Nineveh's sin, He is waiting for a (one) man to become obedient and willing to proclaim His message to the nation.[8]

> *And I sought for a man among them, that should make up the hedge, and stand in the gap before me for the land, that I should destroy it: but I found none.*
>
> Ezekiel 22: 30

> *Therefore He said that He would destroy them, had not Moses His chosen stood before Him in the BREACH, to turn away His wrath, lest He should destroy them.*
>
> Psalm 106:23

President William Jefferson Clinton, it is time to get serious. This country needs a Moses for today.

Billy Sunday
Billy Graham
Billy Clinton ?
(God works in mysterious ways!)

By now my self-righteous Christian friends are clutching their hearts. However, while driving around Los Angeles one afternoon this thought came in like a flash...Bill Clinton...evangelist. Ironically, shortly after that I read that Billy Graham made the statement that you would make a great evangelist (see last sentence of page 113). God is about to take you on a great adventure, enjoy the ride!

[8] Excerpt from Nineveh's Repentance and Deliverance — Page 149

84

Regarding my earlier comments concerning the ills of the country, I said all that to say...the agenda of the "powers that be" will come to pass regardless of what we do, IT'S IN THE BOOK. According to scripture things are going to get worse before they get better. Those that have been set apart for the work of the "end times" will get through it with the protection and guidance of the Holy Spirit. It is very difficult to sit back and watch the country, in fact the world, go to hell in a handbasket (as my Grandmother would have said), however, we can take comfort in knowing God has it under control and His Master Plan is being fulfilled. What an exciting time to be alive! Revelations is unfolding!

Alan Nelson (AJ), a true prophet of God, has mentioned several times that in these last days, God is going to raise up the little children and have them speak words of wisdom for the Kingdom of God. When AJ was speaking one night, in a church in southern California, he was talking about a letter that was sent to you by a little nine year old girl, named Cassia. Thanks to AJ, I was able to get a copy of the letter from Cassia herself. Just in case it never made it to your desk in the White House, it is printed for you on the next page. Below is a note from her father:

"At that time Jesus answered and said, I thank thee, 0 Father, Lord of heaven and earth, because thou hast hid these things from the wise and prudent, and host revealed them unto babes." (Matthew 11:25)

Just the other day, my second oldest daughter, Cassia, handed me a letter that she felt compelled to write and send to President Clinton. As a father, I'm constantly praying and instructing my children to arise and fulfill their God-given destiny to possess the gates of their enemies (Psalms 127:3-5). The Lord in His infinite grace constantly gives us signs that He is watching over our children and is answering our prayers for their lives. The following letter to the president is another indication that my children truly desire is to be used of God to make a difference in their generation. Nothing can encourage a father's and mother's heart more than knowing the joy of their children walking in the truth and pursuing their destiny in Christ. Keep in mind that she was not coached by us to write this letter, this was from her very own heart and in her own words to reach out to a man that desperately needs the wisdom that is coming forth from the mouth of babes (Psalms 8:2).

— Rusty Lee Thomas

(Elijah Ministries, Waco, TX)

Dear Mr. president,

I'm nine years old. I have three brothers and three sisters. We are truly Christians. and if I have to I will die for my Lord. Why dont you give your life to Jesus, it will be much better. I Know you dont want To listen to what I'm saying, But you Need to turn and change your ways and Listen. Don't make other people listen for you. I know your secrets God knows your secrets. please listen to me, this is going to be Verry Important for you sooner or later. My dad is a minister His name is Rusty Lee Thomas. Well I've got to go, please change and give your life To God.

Cassia thomas
p.s. Jesus loves you!

President Clinton, God has given you many gifts and more charisma than one man needs. Where ever you are and what ever may happen in your political career, be content in your circumstances while going through the fire knowing God's purpose for it all will unfold in His perfect time. You have a major part to play in God's end time plan. He is your judge, jury and attorney. Don't look to the left or the right, keep focused on Him and He will lead and guide you in humility. A humble President will humble his people and therefore humble the nation. When you humble yourself and forget about being a politician, God Almighty will exalt you and you will walk in the role of statesman (or evangelist). Be a mouthpiece for your Creator, that is the high calling.

> *I press toward the mark for the prize of the high calling of God in Christ Jesus.*
>
> Philippians 3:14

He is waiting and listening for that humble cry...

So...Help Me God!

May the Grace & Mercy of Our Lord Be With You,

April Shenandoah

P.S. You have the best counselor, consultant, mentor and friend sitting on Capital Hill right now. He is a faithful, trustworthy, spirit-filled, wise man of God, the Chaplain of the Senate, Dr. Lloyd J. Ogilvie. God ordained him for that position before the foundation of the earth, as He did you for President. If you two are not already personally attached I beseech you to connect yourself with one of the greatest men to ever grace Washington, D.C.

A Prayer For:

The President
Of the United States

From: *Prayers That Prevail for America*

Key Thought: No leader can go forward any faster than the people will follow.

Key Scripture: *"I exhort therefore, that, first of all, supplications, prayers, intercessions, and giving of thanks, be made for all men; For kings, and for all that are in authority; that we may lead a quiet and peaceable life in all godliness and honesty"* (1 *Tim. 2:1-2*).

Prayer: Heavenly Father, I come before you in the mighty name of Jesus Christ. Thank you, Father, for your servant, **Bill Clinton**, the President of the United States of America. it is comforting and re-assuring to know that his heart is in your hands and, like the rivers of water, you turn it in whatever directions you choose.[1]

Lord, I beseech you to turn our president's heart in the direction of all your ways, because your way is perfect, your, Word is tried, and you are a buckler to all those who trust in you.[2]
Father, I Pray for the president that if he does not have a personal relationship with Jesus Christ, that he would be converted,[3] receive Jesus as his Lord,[4] and be born again by your Spirit.[5]
I pray, if the president is saved, that you would draw him ever closer to you and work in him by your Spirit to will and to do your good pleasure.[6] I ask that as he has therefore received Christ Jesus the Lord, that he would walk in Him; rooted and built up in Him, established in the faith as he has been taught, and abound therein with thanksgiving.[7]

Grant him a spirit of wisdom and revelation in the knowledge of you, the eyes of his understanding being enlightened that he may know the hope of your calling and what is the riches of the glory of your inheritance in the saints and what is the exceeding greatness of your power to him who believes.[8]

I ask that you strengthen him with might by your Spirit in the inner man: that Christ may dwell in his heart through faith; that he being rooted and grounded in love may comprehend with all saints what is the breadth, length, depth and height, and know the love of Christ, which surpasses knowledge and be filled with all of your fullness, O God.[9]

Father, let the seeds of your Word that have been sown in his heart find good ground and spring up in a fruitful harvest of righteousness, godliness and salvation.[10]

Grant unto him the wisdom that is from above – true wisdom that is first pure, then peaceable, gentle, and easy to be entreated, full of good fruits, without partiality, and without hypocrisy.[11]

Establish him in your wisdom and your righteousness. Let your Word be a lamp unto his feet and a light unto his path.[12] He who rules over men must be just, ruling in the fear of God.[13] Father, bless our president with wisdom and justice that come from reverently fearing you. Remind him that the fear of the Lord is the beginning of knowledge,[14] and that whosoever hearkens unto you shall dwell safely, and shall be quiet from fear of evil.[15]

Provide the President with the power and skills he needs to be a peacemaker in his relationships with other leaders, the Congress of the United States and all other people. Lord Jesus, you showed us in all other areas, by declaring, "Blessed are the peacemakers: for they shall be called the children of God."[16] May he be so filled with Peace and the ways of peace that others will see him as your child and desire to follow his example.

Father, protect our President from all evil as he deals with the issues of an evil and adulterous generation.[17] By his submission to you may many others realize the importance of submission to the governing authorities, for we realize that there is no authority but yours, and the authorities that be are ordained by you.[18]

Give our president the courage,[19] wisdom, knowledge, discretion and understanding to disentangle himself from any unholy alliances formed in the political process.[20] Let all such alliances be cut off and their effects destroyed.[21] Let all righteous alliances flourish and prosper for the blessing of the president and of America.[22]

Bless the president and his family with all spiritual blessings in heavenly places in Christ. Thank you for choosing him before the foundation of the world.[23] Bless his vice president, **Al Gore**, and his family with your spiritual graces and gifts.

Teach your people, Lord, to Pray for our leaders so that we may lead a quiet and peaceable life in all godliness and honesty,[24] and help us to be thankful for them. Give us a full realization of the importance of prayer for our leaders and for our nation because this is a key to revival and change in our land. Remind us of your Word which says that if your people, which are called by your name, will humble themselves, and pray, and seek your face, and turn from their wicked ways, then you will hear from heaven, and forgive our sin and heal our land.[25]

Fill the White House with the light of your presence, Lord. You give salvation unto kings.[26] and you deliver your people from the sword. Lead our president, his family and the citizens of our country to become the light of the world, a city set upon a hill that cannot be hid.[27]

For our president and his family, I ask that you cover them with your feathers and under your wings may they learn to trust. May your truth be their shield and buckler. Let no evil befall them and give your angels charge over them to keep them in all their ways.[28]

Draw the president to you, Father, and fill his heart with your Spirit and your love that he might set his love on you. Deliver him and set him on high because he knows your name. And as he calls upon you, give him the answers he needs in all his decision-making. Let him know that you will be with him in the time of trouble. Satisfy him with long life and show him your salvation.[29]

References: (1)Proverbs 21:1; (2)Psalms 18:30; (3)Acts 3:19; (4)Romans 10:9-10; (5)John 3:5- 7; (6)Philippians 2:13; (7) Colossians 2:6-7; (8)Ephesians 1:17-19; (9)Ephesians 3:16-19; (10)Luke 8:11-15; (11)James 3:17; (12)Psalms 119:105; (13)2 Samuel 23:3; (14)Proverbs 1:7; (15)Proverbs 1:33, (16)Matthew 5:9; (17)Matthew 12:39; (18)Romans 13:1; (19)Joshua 1:7; (20)Proverbs 2:10-15; (21)Psalms 10:15; (22)Psalms 72:7; (23)Ephesians 1:4; (24)1 Timothy 2:1-3; (25)2 Chronicles 7:14; (26)Psalms 144:10; (27)Matthew 5:14; (28)Psalms 91:4,10-11; (29)Psalms 91:14-16.

Prayer taken from *Prayers That Prevail for America*, Published by Victory House, Inc., Tulsa, OK. Used with permission of the publisher.

Virginia Kelly

The Star-Spangled Banner

The American national anthem, officially designated by Congress in 1931, was written to the tune of Anacreon in Heaven, an 18th century drinking song which served as the hymn of the Anacreontic Society of London. It was probably composed by an English musician, John Stafford Smith, but was applied to many songs, including R. T. Paine's patriotic ode, Adams and Liberty, in 1798.

During the War of 1812, Francis Scott Key, a young American lawyer, went to the British fleet off Baltimore to exchange prisoners under a flag of truce, and from this vantage point was compelled to witness, throughout the night of September 12, 1814, the British bombardment of Fort McHenry. With the first rays of dawn and after the firing had ceased, he saw the flag still proudly waving. Under the inspiration of this dramatic moment, Francis Scott Key penned the immortal words for the three stanzas of *The Star Spangled Banner*.

"Oh, — say! can you see — by the dawn's early light,
What so proudly we hail'd at the twi-light's last gleaming,
Whose broad stripes and bright stars, through the perilous fight,
O'er the ramparts we watch'd were so gallantly streaming?
And the rocket's red glare, the bombs bursting in air,
Gave proof through the night that our flag was still there.
Oh — say, does the Star-Spangled Banner — yet — wave —
O'er the land — of the free and the home of the brave.

"On the shore, dimly seen through the mists of the deep,
Where the foe's haughty host in dread silence reposes,
What is that which the breeze, o'er the towering steep,
As it fitfully blows, half conceals, half discloses?
Now it catches the gleam of the morning's first beam,
In full glory reflected now shines on the stream.
'Tis the Star-Spangled Banner. On, long may it wave —
O'er the land — of the free and the home of the brave.

"Oh — thus be it ever, when — free men shall stand,
Between their lov'd homes and war's desolation!
Blest with victory and peace, may the Heav'n rescued land,
Praise the Pow'r that hath made and preserv'd us a nation!
And conquer we must, when our cause it is just,
And this be our motto: "In God is our trust."
Oh — say, does the Star-Spangled Banner in triumph shall wave
O'er the land — of the free and the home of the brave."

America the Beautiful

Katherine Lee Bates (1859-1929) In 1892, she wrote the famous patriotic song, *America the Beautiful* after seeing the inspiring view atop Pike's Peak in Colorado. This song was so popular that it almost became the National Anthem of the United States in 1920.

O Beautiful for Spacious Skies,
For Amber Waves of Grain,
For Purple Mountain Majesties,
Above the Fruited Plain!

America! America!
God Shed His Grace on Thee
And Crowned Thy Good with Brotherhood
From Sea to Shining Sea!

O Beautiful for Pilgrims Feet,
Whose Stern Impassioned Stress
A Thoroughfare for Freedom Beat
Across the Wilderness!

America! America!
God Mend Thy Every Flaw,
Confirm Thy Soul in Self-Control
Thy Liberty in Law!

O Beautiful for Heroes Proved
In Liberating Strife,
Who More Than Self Their Country Loved,
And Mercy More Than Life!

America! America!
May God Thy Gold Refine
Till All Success Be Nobleness
And Every Gain Divine!

O Beautiful for Patriots Dream
That sees Beyond the Years
Thine Alabaster Cities Gleem
Undimmed by Human Tears!

America! America!
God Shed His Grace on Thee
And Crowned Thy Good with Brotherhood
From Sea to Shining Sea!

FootNotes:

Articles
and
Documents

The Bible:

Rock of Our Republic

Providence Foundation

The Bible: Rock of Our Republic

On June 8, 1845, President Andrew Jackson said that "the Bible is the rock on which our Republic rests." Early Americans would almost universally agree that the religious, social, educational, and political life of America was primarily shaped by the Bible.

Our states were colonized by people who desired to freely worship the God of the Bible; our schools were begun so that everyone would be able to read and understand the Bible for themselves; our universities were founded to train ministers who were knowledgeable of the Scriptures; our laws and constitutions were written based on Biblical ideas; and our founding fathers overwhelmingly had a Biblical worldview.

Most Americans today have not been taught this important truth, even though many still recognize it. Even *Newsweek* magazine, on December 26, 1982, acknowledged that: "Now historians are discovering that the Bible, perhaps even more than the Constitution is our Founding document." It used to be common knowledge that America's Biblical foundation produced America's freedom, justice, and prosperity. In recent generations America has been shifting from a Biblical foundation to a humanistic foundation, where the God of the Bible is being replaced by man as god. The result has been the decay of society and loss of liberty. Noah Webster wrote:

"The moral principles and precepts contained in the Scriptures ought to form the basis of all our civil constitutions and laws. All the miseries and evils which men suffer from vice, crime, ambition, injustice, oppression, slavery, and war, proceed from their despising or neglecting the precepts contained in the Bible."

For the good of America we must once again restore the Bible to the central role it played in shaping this nation. To do this we must first understand that role. Following is a brief outline examining the influence of the Bible in our history.

1.   The Bible was the single most important influence in the lives of colonial Americans.

Lawrence A. Cremin writes:

"Above all, the colonists were acquainted with the Bible itself, principally in the Geneva Version but increasingly in the King James Version. The Bible was read and recited, quoted and consulted early committed to memory and constantly searched for meaning. Deemed universally relevant, it remained throughout the century the single most important cultural influence in the lives of Anglo-Americans. . . . Though the Bible had been richly valued for generations, it was not until the seventeenth century that it was widely read and studied. The message of Protestantism was that men could find in Scripture the means to salvation, the keys to good and evil, the rules by which to live, and the standards against which to measure the conduct of prince and pastor."

New England of the 1700s was described by historian George Bancroft in this way:

"In the settlements which grew up in the interior, on the margin of the greenwood, the plain meeting-house of the congregation for public worship was everywhere the central point, near it stood the public school The snug farm-houses, owned as freehold, without quit-rents, were dotted along the way. In every hand was the Bible; every home was a house of prayer; all had been taught, many had comprehended, a methodical theory of the divine purpose in creation, and of the destiny of man."

A.   The Aitken Bible

Prior to America's independence almost every house in the colonies possessed and cherished the English Bible, yet, no English Bibles had ever been printed in the colonies (some had been printed in German and native Indian languages). It would have been piracy to do so. Only after independence were English Bibles printed. When the war cut off the supply of English Bibles, the Congress, in September 1777, resolved to import 20,000 Bibles from Scotland, Holland or elsewhere because "the use of the Bible is so universal and its importance so great." In 1782, Congress acted the role of a Bible society by officially approving the printing and distribution of the "Bible of the Revolution," an American translation prepared by Robert Aitken.

B.   Oath of Office taken on the Bible

At the first Presidential Inauguration George Washington laid his hand on the Bible and took the oath of office as prescribed by the Constitution, adding the words "so help me God," after which he leaned over and reverently kissed the Bible. Washington then went to the Senate and read his inaugural address. After this they all walked to St. Paul's Chapel for prayers and a service. All the presidents have taken the oath of office on the Bible.

II.   The People who settled America were people of the book. *Sola sctiptura* was their motto.

A majority of the settlers of America were a product of the Protestant Reformation. The major impetus of this reform was the Bible being translated into the common languages of the people. Throughout Europe the people read the Scriptures and began looking to them as the standard by which they judged not only their own actions but also that of priest and king. The Bible became the source of their ideas and principles. This brought many trials and persecutions and forced many to flee their native countries to America.

Many of those who had paved the way for settlement were inspired by the Scriptures as well. Composed in 1502 after his third voyage, Columbus' *Book of Prophecies* reveals he felt he was fulfilling a divine mission through his voyages. This work contains hundreds of prophetic passages of Scripture that Columbus related to his great enterprise. The man most responsible for the English colonization of America was a minister, Richard Hakluyt. He said he was first inspired by the Scriptures to promote colonization. His chief motive was to extend God's Kingdom throughout the earth.

Some of the early settlers:

1.   Pilgrims

They were enlightened by the Word of God and sought to live according to its precepts. Pastor to the Pilgrims, John Robinson, wrote in his farewell letter:

"I charge you, before God and his blessed angels, that you follow me no farther than you have seen me follow the Lord Jesus Christ. The Lord has more truth yet to break forth out of his holy word. I cannot sufficiently bewail the condition of the reformed churches, who are come to a period in religion, and will go at present no farther than the instruments of their reformation. Luther and Calvin were great and shining lights in their times, yet they penetrated not into the whole counsel of God. I beseech you, remember it -'tis an article of your church covenant - that you be ready to receive whatever truth shall be made known to you from the written word of God."

2.   Puritans

The early settlers of Salem, Massachusetts were typical of the many Puritans who came to America. One reason they came was to "wynne the natives to the Christian faith." During their voyage from England they "constantly served God, morning and evening, by reading and expounding a chapter in the Bible, singing and prayer."

The First Charter of Massachusetts (1629) states the desire that all the inhabitants would "be so religiously, peaceably, and civilly governed, as their good life and orderly conversation may win and incite the natives of country to the knowledge and obedience of the only true God and Savior of mankind, and the Christian faith, which in Our royal intention and the adventurers' free profession, is the Principal end of this plantation ......"

The center of the seal of the colony of Massachusetts Bay shows an Indian speaking the words, "Come Over And Help Us." The work of John Eliot "Apostle to the Indians," and Daniel Gookin, a civil magistrate and superintendent to the Indians, shows how many of the early settlers desired to bring the gospel to the native Americans - how they did come over to help them. These two men worked for over 40 years to evangelize and civilize the Algonquin Indians of Massachusetts. Eliot constantly traveled to various Indians villages and taught them the gospel. When many began to be converted he set up "Praying Towns" where these Christian Indians could live out their new life in Christ and learn how to separate themselves from their pagan way of life. In these towns, which came to number fourteen, the Indians were self-governed and self-supporting. Twenty-four of these Christian Indians became ministers in order to carry on the work of the gospel among their own people. Hundreds attended schools and some attended Harvard College.

Eliot believed that the Indians needed the Bible in their own language in order to truly grow in the complete liberty of the gospel, both internally and externally, both personally and civilly. Therefore, after learning the native Indian language, he developed a written language for the Algonquin tongue, as none existed. He then worked for twelve years on translating the Bible, while continuing his pastoral duties in the church in Roxbury and regularly traveling to minister to the Indians. He completed the work in 1658. The Algonquin Bible was first published in 1661-1663 with funds primarily contributed by Englishmen. This was the first Bible printed in America.

3.   Scotch-Irish Presbyterians

Many settled on the western frontiers of Pennsylvania, Maryland, Virginia, and North Carolina. At every place they "had their pastor, and trained their children in Bible truth, in the catechism, obedience to parents, - a wholesome doctrine practically enforced by all the colonists, and reverence for the Sabbath and its sacred duties."

4.   Georgia colonists

Some of the earliest settlers to Georgia were German Lutherans who were driven out of their country when they refused to renounce their Protestant faith, and were invited by the Society in England for Propagating the Gospel to emigrate to Savannah. George Bancroft writes: "On the last day of October 1733, 'the evangelical community,' well supplied with Bibles and hymn-books, catechisms and books of devotion. . . after a discourse and prayer and benedictions, cheerfully, and in the name of God, began their pilgrimage." They arrived at Charleston on March 18, 1734 and were welcomed by Oglethorpe.

III.   The Bible formed the basis of America's civil laws.

1.   Jamestown

Between 1609 and 1612 a set of laws was drawn up for the colony of Virginia. In these *Laws Divine, Morall and Martiall, etc.* the colonists were required to serve God, to attend divine services, to not speak against God or blaspheme God's holy name, and to not speak or act in any way that would "tend to the derision, or despight [open defiance] of Gods holy word upon paine of death."

While this may seem extreme to us today, it nonetheless reveals their desire to live according to God's commands.

In 1619 the first Representative Assembly of the new world met in the Church in Jamestown. It was begun by prayer. One of the resolves of this body was to encourage the farmers and plantation owners to open their homes to Indian youth with the purpose of converting them to Christianity and teaching them the precepts of God's Word.

2. The Laws of the Pilgrims

The Pilgrims believed that God and His word were the supreme source of all authority. Their compilation of laws during the 1600s clearly revealed this. Their *Book of General Laws (1671)* begins by stating that "Laws... are so far good and wholesome, as by how much they are derived from, and agreeable to the ancient Platform of Gods Law. As one reads through these laws it is obvious they looked to the Bible to assist them in formulating good and wholesome laws. They even gave Scriptural references to support their capital laws.

3. Fundamental Orders of Connecticut

This first American constitution was written by Rev. Thomas Hooker in 1638. The oath imposed on the magistrates bound them to "to administer justice according to the laws here established, and for want thereof according to the rule of the word of God. " The oath of the governor (and similarly the Magistrate) ended with these words: "I... will further the execution of Justice according to the rule of Gods word; so help me God, in the name of the Lord Jesus Christ."

4. New Haven Colony

Established in 1638 under the guidance of Rev. John Davenport, this colony rested its frame of government on a covenant providing that "all of them would be ordered by the rules which the scriptures held forth to them." God's word was established as the only rule in public affairs. Bancroft wrote that "New Haven made the Bible its statutebook."

5. Massachusetts Body of Liberties

Written in 1641 by Rev. Nathaniel Ward, the Pentateuch (the first five books of the Bible) was the basis for its criminal code, and "in case of the defect of a law in any partecular case" the standard was "the word of God." Article 65 states: "No custome or prescription shall ever prevail amongst us in any moral cause, our meaning is to maintain anything that can be proved to be morally sinful by the word of god." The capital laws in the Body of Liberties give numerous scriptures as justification for carrying out the death penalty.

6. Arbitrary Government Described (1644)

In explaining how the government of Massachusetts was to work, Governor John Winthrop wrote: "By these it appears, that the officers of this body politic have a rule to walk by in all their administrations, which rule is the Word of God, and such conclusions and deductions as are, or shall be regularly drawn from thence."

7. Code of the Connecticut General Court, 1650

No man's life, liberty, or property was to be taken except by specific law established and sufficiently published by the General Court (the legislature), "or in case of the defect of a law, in any particular case, by the Word of God."

The Connecticut Code of Law lists several crimes receiving the death penalty. Specific scriptures are listed as justification for these capital laws. For example:

4. If any person shall commit any willful murder, which is manslaughter, committed upon

malice, hatred, or cruelty, not in a man necessary and just defense, nor by mere casualty against his will, he shall be put to death. Ex. 21:12-14; Num. 35:30,31.

10. If any man steals a man or mankind. he shall be put to death. Ex. 21:16

The Code also states that "the open contempt of God's Word, and messengers thereof, is the desolating sin of civil states and churches..."

Many other early constitutions, compacts, charters, and laws could be examined that reveal the central role of the Bible in shaping America's civil documents, such as the Charter of Rhode Island, the Frame of Government of Pennsylvania, the Declaration of Independence, various state constitutions, and the U.S. Constitution and Bill of Rights.

Printed by permission from the Providence Foundation
PO Box 6759, Charlottesville, Virginia 22906

The Elijah Report:

The Militant Patriot Movement

Ascension Ministries

The Militant Patriot Movement

The "Militant Patriot Movement" is preparing to defend themselves from the New World Order (NWO) by taking up arms against it. Preservation of the flesh is the underlying motive in their desire to return our government to the way it was. They defend the United States Constitution as if it had been canonized into being the 67th book of the Bible, and refuse to hear what the Bible teaches about their actions.

Their claim is that our government is unjust and therefore we do not need to submit to it, and if necessary, we will overthrow the government in order to preserve our flesh. We must understand that today is not the first time that God's people have had to submit to unrighteous rulers and their governments. *(However, it will be the last - praise God).*

Almost all the Old Testament prophets served and/or submitted to unrighteous authorities without taking up arms against them.   The apostles and the whole of the first century church followed this pattern even at the risk of having their property confiscated, physical imprisonment and/or death (Heb. 10:32-39, Acts 7:54-60; 8: 1-4; 23:1-5, Rom. 13). Even Jesus was in submission to the unrighteous government of Rome and its leaders, because their authority was given to them by God (John 19:9-1 1).

In Romans 13, Paul wrote to the church in Rome, and told them to submit to the governing authorities of what was then the NWO of their time, the Roman Empire. Paul does not qualify submission to authority based on governments beingjust or unjust, but on God's sovereignty that established those rulers to serve His purposes.

However, we must understand that submission to government authority does not always translate into obedience to government authority. Listed below are the only circumstances in scripture, that I am familiar with, in which God seems to allow disobedience to government authority.

1) When we are forced to worship images, idols or other God's (Dan. 3).
2) When forced to stop praying to Jehovah, the God of the Bible (Dan. 6).
3) When forced to stop preaching in the name of Jesus (Acts 5:27-32).
4) When forced to give our children up (Ex. 2: 1 -IO, Luke 2:13 -15).
5) When forced to take the "mark of the beast" (Rev. 13:11-18).

Please note that in none of these instances does God ever release anyone to take up arms against the governing authorities to defend themselves. That's because the Body of Christ is called to love even its enemies, bless those who curse us and pray for those who despitefully use us. Jesus said that this was how we would know that we are *"the children of God"* (Matt. 5:44, Luke 6:32-37).

The fear of man is greater in the "Militant Patriot Movement" than the fear of God. And I would submit to any one, that if you hate Bill Clinton or any other governing authorities to the point of taking up arms against them, then you may not be a child of God. Selah!

The History of Revolutions

Let's talk about revolutions and historical events. The major revolutions in the world all overthrew and replaced unjust rulers and their governments. The Russian, French, and American revolutions all began with militias who believed that they were advancing the cause of personal freedom. But in reality, they were all part of the plan of ancient secret societies to move nations toward their NWO.

The Russian revolution was supposedly to redistribute the wealth to the peasants and make all men truly equal. Not only did that not happen, but the new form of government, called communism, was far more oppressive than the Czars. Those people who fought and died for Mother Russia were patriots. They believed they were going to do a better job of running their country than those who were in power under the monarchy.

What has been the result of this patriotic revolution? Russia has come to a place where she has wasted most of her resources. Manufacturing output is low, food production does not meet the needs of the population, their financial system has failed, and the NWO has Russia right where it wants them, in dependence upon the other NWO countries of the world for food-and finances.

In 1924, from his deathbed, Lenin said "I committed a great error. My nightmare is to have the feeling that I'm lost in an ocean of blood from the innumerable victims. It is too late to return. To save our country, Russia, we would have needed men like Francis of Assisi. With ten men like him we would have saved Russia." Many of the Russian patriots were among the 40,000,000 killed by Stalin in his fear of further rebellion. Remember, those who live by the sword must die by the sword.

The French revolution in particular should give warning to any self proclaimed patriot of the result of taking up arms against his government. France had the best standard of living in the world at the time of the French Revolution. The king of France at that time was insensitive and cruel at best. A small group began to clamor for the overthrow of the French monarchy. They were funded and led by the German Illuminati and the Jacobin Club, both were made up of Freemasons. These patriots wore emblems on their hats that looked like little targets. In retrospect that seems appropriate. Many well meaning men were drawn into giving their lives to this fight.

After the aristocrats were killed or chased out of the country and order was restored, these patriots were either used as cannon fodder in the elite's failed attempt at global conquest, or they were imprisoned as a threat to the State. Tle result of this historical event was a dramatic change in the government structures of all of Europe. The globalists now had western Europe firmly in its grip.

The American Revolution had high ideals just as did the other revolutions in history. The patriots of that time believed they fought for life, liberty, and the pursuit of happiness. Their heartfelt faith in Jesus as Savior and Lord was a fact. But great deception was at the core of that revolt. According to the 1951 Masonic edition of the Holy Bible, twenty-four of George Washington's major generals were Masons. Thirty of his thirty-three brigadier generals were Masons. Of the fifty-six signers of the Declaration of Independence, fifty-three were Freemasons. According to the Masonic publication, New Age, "It was the Masons who brought about the war, and it was the Masonic generals who carried it through to a successful conclusion. In fact, the famous Boston Tea Party, which precipitated the war, was actually a recessed meeting of a Masonic Lodge."

This does not mean that all our founding fathers were part of some evil conspiracy and willingly participated in the 'great plan' of the secret societies. What this does mean is the underlying goal of the American Revolution, was to move the world closer to the NWO's one world government. The purpose, of which, is to establish the structure for the rule of the Antichrist. That structure now seems to be emerging in our time as the United Nations.

God Himself Will Destroy The NWO

Most patriots are honest and sincere people who love America. Unfortunately they are playing right into the plans of the globalists. The NWO is using them as a key ingredient of their strategy to bring about an armed revolution in this country.

Before a 1941 Senate Subcommittee, James P. Warburg said, "We will have world government whether or not we like it. The question is, will it come by consent or by conquest?" Their plan is to force the patriots into a fight, and that's when they will take this country by whatever force is necessary. I am talking about their use of conventional, biological and even nuclear weapons if they deem it necessary, and they probably will.

There is no way to win a physical fight with the NWO, because God has ordained for the NWO (Mystery Babylon) to come to power (Rev. 17:17). Once it is fully established, and the Antichrist is ruling it (Rev. 13: 5-7), God is going to judge it on behalf of His people (Rev. 18:20).

Speaking through the prophet Daniel, God makes it very clear that the antichrist and his NWO kingdom "... *will be broken (destroyed) without human agency (intervention)...* " and that the horn (antichrist) will "...*wage war with the saints and overpowering them until the Ancient of days (Jesus) (comes), and judgment (will be) passed in favor of the saints of the Highest One, and the time arrived when the saints (will take) possession of the kingdom "* (Dan. 8:25; 7:21-22).

What we are talking about here is the end of this current age and the beginning of the Millennial kingdom of Jesus the Messiah. That's nothing to be fearful of, but something we should be looking forward to. So before you join any patriot movement, that is trying to preserve a kingdom of this world (the U.S.), ask yourself: What am I a patriot of? Do I support the preservation of the kingdoms of this world, or do I support the coming of the Kingdom of God?

Advancing the Kingdom of God

The Bible teaches very clearly that the kingdom of God and the kingdoms of this world are at war. The question is; How do we identify and support the advancement of the kingdom of God and not the kingdoms of this world?

Paul speaks about this war, and in his instructions on how to fight it he says, *"...the weapons of our warfare are not of the flesh, "* and that, *"...our struggle is not against flesh and blood, but against the powers, against the world forces of this darkness, against the spiritual forces of wickedness in the heavenly places"* (2 Cor. 10:4, Gal. 6:12). This would seem to indicate that we can not preserve or advance the kingdom of God by physical force.

Jesus said, *"My kingdom is not of this (physical) world, "* but that, *"...it is in (us) "* (John 18:36, Luke 17:20-2 1). The only thing that is in us, that wasn't in us before we were saved, is the Spirit of God. Therefore, advancing the kingdom of God has to do with the manifestation of His Spirit to set the captives free (Luke 4:17-19). Jesus best describes the manifestation of the kingdom of God when He said, *"If I cast out demons by the Spirit of God, then the kingdom of God **has come** unto you"* (Matt. 12:28).

Just as Jesus was called to reveal the kingdom of God through powerful signs and wonders, so are we called to do those same works of the Spirit, and even greater works. That's the kingdom of God, not armed revolution.

Simply put, if your plan is to take up arms in the carnal revolution to preserve the kingdoms of this world, you are operating in the flesh and your defeat has already been recorded in God's Word (Rev. 13:10). But if you are pressing into the revelation that the kingdom of God is the manifestation of the power of the Holy Spirit to set those who are in spiritual bondage free, then you will be part of the glorious day when *"...the kingdoms of this world (have) become the kingdom of our Lord, and of His Christ; and He shall reign for ever and ever"* (Rev. II: 15).

Don't miss it!   **TER**

"Jesus said to him, 'Put your sword back in its place; for all those who take up the sword shall perish by the sword."
Matt. 26:52

"You shall not speak evil of a ruler of your people."
Ex. 22:28 Acts 23:6

"the Most High is ruler over the realm of mankind, and bestows it on whomever He wishes."
Dan. 4:25

Reprinted from the Elijah Report, May/June 1996. Printed by permission from Ascension Ministries
1409 E Olive Ct, #A, Ft Collins, Colorado 80524

Breakfast Meeting Report:

Standing in the Gap

California Constitution
Education Committee

Gerald Nordskog

Standing "In The Gap"

Dear Good Reader,

A dozen evangelical leaders met at the White House for breakfast with President Clinton on October 18, last year. Those attending included V. P. Al Gore, Jack Hayford (Church On The Way), Bill Hybels (Willow Creek Community Church), Richard Mouw (Fuller Seminary's president), Eugene Habecker (American Bible Society), Bob Seiple (World Vision), Mark Noll (Wheaton College), Roberta Hestenes (Eastern College president), Tony Campolo (sociology professor), Jay Kesler (Taylor University president), Jesse Miranda (Azusa Pacific University professor), Philip Yancey (Christianity Today columnist, author), and John Perkins (Christian Community Development Assn.).

Rus Walton, SCCEC Associate and Exec. Director of Plymouth Rock Foundation, relates: "Ms. Hestenes reported that Clinton 'knows his Bible' (indeed, so does Satan; the question is not 'does he know God's word?' but 'does he seek to obey it?').

John Perkins said the fact that Clinton expresses his faith differently "from many evangelicals, that is not the issue."

Walton continued, "To Plymouth Rock Foundation (& SCCEC), obedience to God and laws on all things including such matters as abortion, sodomy, euthanasia, state vs. parental child care and education, etc. is indeed "the issue."

"BY THEIR FRUITS YOU SHALL KNOW THEM..." Yes, we are told to pray for those in authority (including the Clintons). But, we must also pray that they will repent, and reform!

And, it does not mean we are to be politically "correct" and compromise our faith or soften our Bible-based stand on God's law-word. Just Whom do we seek to please? What is the price of being popular? (Gal. 1:10). We who are His are to have no truck with the Ahabs or Jezebels.

Texe Marrs (Living Truth Ministries) reports: "When Clinton asked the assembled Christian leaders for advice on what he could do to better the spiritual climate of America, not one person present brought up the issues of abortion or homosexuality. Instead, these so-called 'Christian' evangelicals uniformly lavished praise on the President. Jack Hayford gushingly told Mr. Clinton that God had given him a 'vision' that Clinton would be a great president.

"Tony Campolo thanked the President," continued Texe Marrs, "for his humane policies and assured Mr. Clinton that he is held in highest regard by 'moderate' Christians. There were smiles all around. Later, Campolo stated that the President is 'an evangelical Christian who wants to be religious.' Clinton, he said, is getting a raw deal from mean and cruel Christians who gleefully rejoice at any lie that might hurt the dignity of our leaders.' Campolo insisted that Clinton is a 'loving friend' of all Christians, and branded those who oppose the President's policies as filled with 'hate.'

According to Marrs, "It was also revealed that the evangelicals who met privately with Clinton had agreed in advance not to ask any embarrassing questions about the President's support of gay rights and abortion. That would be divisive, they concluded, so the group focused instead on milder topics such as volunteerism' and the 'inner-city poor.'

"Meanwhile," continued Marrs, "evangelist Billy Graham was separately quoted in the press as being extremely pleased with the performance in office of his friend, Bill Clinton. **'Bill Clinton would make a great evangelist,'** Graham glowingly assured the national press corps.

Printed by permission from the Southern California Constitution Education Committee
Ventura Harbor, California, USA.

Biblical Principles:

Accountability

Plymouth Rock Foundation

PRIN'CI'PLE. *n* [L. *prin-cipium*, begining], a truth; that which supports an assertion, an action, or a series of actions: a law comprehending many subordinate truths.

BIBLICAL *Prin'ci'ples*

One in a series published in the service of The King by PLYMOUTH ROCK FOUNDATION, Marlborough NH 03455/1-800-210-1620

ACCOUNTABILITY

AC-COUNT-ABIL.I.TY, n subject to giving account: answerable. The state of being liable to answer for one's conduct; liability to give account and to receive reward or punishment for actions. Every man is accountable to God for his conduct. (See responsibility)

The Biblical Principle

Accountability is a basic Biblical principle. Each individual counts (Matt 10.29-31), and is accountable (Luke 21:36).

From the beginning, from the first Adam, accountability has been a key part of God's plan for man and society.

There in the garden, what rule did The Lord God, The Creator of all things, establish for Adam whom He created in His own image?

"Of every tree of the garden you may freely eat: But of the tree of the knowledge of good and evil, you shall not eat of it: for in that day that you eat thereof you shall surely die" (Gen 2:16,17).

This do and live, saith The Lord. That do and die. Adam was accountable. And, did he seek to avoid accountability? Indeed, he did. He sought to shift the blame to Eve. And, what of Eve? Did she not pass the accountability along? *"The devil made me do it!"* (Gen 3.-13)

It did not work for Adam. It did not work for Eve. God held them accountable - both of them, and also the serpent! (Gen 2:14-19). For every act there is an accounting. That which God has created in His image, He holds accountable.

"For you are bought with a price; therefore glorify God in your body, and in your spirit which are God's" (I Cor 6.20).

Years later, when Christ walked on earth, what did our Savior say about accountability?

"You have heard that it was said by them of old time, 'Thou shalt not commit adultery.' But I say unto you, That whosoever looks on a woman to lust after her has committed adultery already with her in his heart" (Matt 5:27,28).

Thus, this we may consider a basic Biblical principle: each and every person is accountable unto The Lord God. For every act and every word (Matt 12-36) and every thought we are accountable to our Creator. Each person, according to the act; and, according to the thought.

Why for every sin thought? Because God knows and judges the heart: out of the heart proceed the thoughts of man (Pr. 4.23). The thought is the seed which bears the act; it is the genesis of the deed. The internal produces the external. To resist the act, avoid the thought. That is why it is so vital to be a "heart" Christian, not just a "mouth" Christian. (see Ps 37:31; Prov. 4:23,23:7a; Matt 5:8, etc.)

Accountability. Throughout God's written word it is a running stream: an abiding promise to those who are faithful; a siren to warn us away from the tides of temptation and the shoals of disobedience; a judgment to those who disobey His laws and deny His word. And, in a strictly temporal scale, it is an essential property if men and nations are to survive.

Nations!

This do and live! That do and die. Men. And, nations.

Yes, nations. The nation which sets other gods before God, the nation *"which will not ... do all the words of the law ... The Lord will make every sickness, and every plague ... until you be destroyed"* (see Deut 28:58-66).

What is the lot of that nation which puts other gods before Him, the nation which rejects The Lord God, *"that [He] should not reign over them"?* I Sam 8:9-117 tells it like it is, even as it is today.

"You shall cry out in that day because of your king (governor/system/bureaucrats) which you shall have chosen you; and The Lord will not hear you in that day" (I Sam 8:18).

Nations, as well as their citizens, are held accountable before God.

Accountability: It brings well-being for the obedient:

"And it shall come to pass, if you shall hearken diligently unto the voice of The Lord your God, to observe and to do all His commandments which I command you this day, that The Lord your God will set you high above all nations of the earth: And all these blessings shall come on you, and overtake you, if you shall obey the voice of The Lord your God. Blessed shall you be in the city, and blessed shall you be in the field. Blessedshall be The fruit of your body (children), *and the fruit of your ground, and the fruit of your cattle, the increase of your kine* (calves), *and the flocks of your sheep. Blessed shall be your basket and your store. Blessed shall you be when you come in and blessed shall you be when you go out* (your routine affairs) (Deut 28:1-6. Read verses 7-14).

Accountability: It brings misery and sorrow for the disobedient:

"But it shall come to pass, if you will not listen unto the voice of The Lord your God, to observe to do all His commandments and His statutes which I command you this day, that all these curses shall come upon you (Deut 28. 15. Read also verses 16-68).

Consider some examples of God's application of accountability to societies, to cities, to nations - and to churches (congregations).

The wickedness of Cain and God's sentence of accountability (Gen 4:8-15). The wickedness of men and accountability through the great flood (Gen 6:5-13; 7:17-24). The destruction of Sodom (Gen 18:20,21;19:1-29). The watery end of Egypt's Pharaoh, who counted himself above and immune to God's power (Ex 6-15:21). The Hebrews whom God freed from bondage but who rejected His purpose and Him (Num 14:20-35). And even Moses, His lawgiver, because of his weak faith (Num 20:8-12; Deut 32:51,52). Or, the accountability for abortion/infanticide (Num 35:330. Or, Ananias and his wife, Saphira (Acts 5:1-11). Or, the accountability of the churches at Ephesus and Smyrna, Pergamos, Thyatira, Sardis, Philadelphia and Laodicea (Rev. 2 & 3).

"I know your works ..." said The Lord. *"I know your works."*

Each and all were held accountable as are even we. God is not mocked! As you sow, so shall you reap. The soul, the church and the nation that sins, it shall be held accountable.

Printed by permission from the Plymouth Rock Foundation
Fisk Mill, PO Box 425, Marlborough, New Hampshire 03455

Whatever You Did Unto One of the Least, You Did Unto Me

Mother Teresa of Calcutta

WHATEVER YOU DID UNTO ONE OF THE LEAST, YOU DID UNTO ME

Mother Teresa of Calcutta (continued from page 48)

of us and bring peace and joy while still in the womb of Mary, Jesus also died on the Cross to show that greater love. He died for you and for me, and for that leper and for that man dying of hunger and that naked person lying in the street, not only of Calcutta, but of Africa, and everywhere. Our Sisters serve these poor people in 105 countries throughout the world. Jesus insisted that we love one another as He loves each one of us. Jesus gave His life to love us and He tells us that we also have to give whatever it takes to do good to one another. And in the Gospel Jesus says very clearly: **"Love as I have loved you."**

Jesus died on the Cross because that is what it took for Him to do good to us - to save us from our selfishness in sin. He gave up everything to do the Father's will - to show us that we too must be willing to give up everything to do God's will – to love one another as He loves each of us. If we are not willing to give whatever it takes to do good to one another, sin is still in us. That is why we too must give to each other until it hurts.

It is not enough for us to say: "I love God," but I also have to love my neighbor. St. John says that you are a liar if you say you love God and you don't love your neighbor. How can you love God whom you do not see, if you do not love your neighbor whom you see, whom you touch, with whom you live? And so it is very important for us to realize that love, to be true, has to hurt. I must be willing to give whatever it takes not to harm other people and, in fact, to do good to them This requires that I be willing to give until it hurts. Otherwise, there is no true love in me and I bring injustice, not peace, to those around me.

It hurt Jesus to love us. We have been created in His image for greater things, to love and to be loved. We must "put on Christ" as Scripture tells us. And so, we have been created to love as He love us. Jesus makes Himself the hungry one, the naked one, the homeless one, the unwanted one, and He says, "You did it to Me." On the last day He will say to those on His right, "whatever you did to the least of these, you did to Me, and He will also say to those on His left, whatever you neglected to do for the least of these, you ne-

glected to do it for Me."

When He was dying on the Cross Jesus said, "I thirst." Jesus is thirsting for our love, and this is the thirst of everyone, poor and rich alike. We all thirst for the love of others, that they go out of their way to avoid harming us and to do good to us. This is the meaning of true love, to give until it hurts.

I can never forget the experience I had in visiting a home where they kept all these old parents of sons and daughters who had just put them into an institution and forgotten them - maybe. I saw that in that home these old people had everything - good food, comfortable place, television, everything, but everyone was looking toward the door. And I did not see a single one with a smile on the face. I turned to Sister and I asked: "Why do these people who have every comfort here, why are they all looking toward the door? Why are they not smiling?"

I am so used to seeing the smiles on our people, even the dying ones smile. And Sister said: "This is the way it is nearly every day. They are expecting, they are hoping that a son or daughter will come to visit them. They are hurt because they are forgotten." And see, this neglect to love brings spiritual poverty. Maybe in our own family we have somebody who is feeling lonely, who is feeling sick, who is feeling worried. Are we there? Are we willing to give until it hurts in order to be with our families, or do we put our own interests first? These are the Questions we must ask ourselves, especially as we begin this year of the family. We must remember that love begins at home and we must also remember that "the future of humanity passes through the family."

I was surprised in the West to see so many young boys and girls given to drugs. And I tried to find out why. Why is it like that, when those in the West have so many more things than those in the East? And the answer was: '

'Because there is no one in the family to receive them.' Our children depend on us for everything - their health, their nutrition, their security, their coming to know and love God. For all of this, they look to us with trust, hope and expectation. But often father and mother are so busy they have no time for their children, or perhaps they are not even married or have given up an their marriage. So the children go to the streets and get involved in drugs or other things. We are talking of love of the child, which is where love and peace must begin. These are the things that break peace.

But I feel that the greatest destroyer of peace today is abortion, because it is a war against the child, a direct killing of the innocent child, murder by the mother herself. And if we accept that a mother can kill even her own child, how can we tell other people not to kill one another? How do we persuade a woman not to have an abortion? As always, we must persuade her with love and we remind ourselves that love means to be willing to give until it hurts. Jesus gave even His life to love us. So, the mother who is thinking of abortion, should be helped to love. that is, to give until it hurts her plans. or her free time, to respect the life of her child. The father of that child, whoever he is, must also give until it hurts.

By abortion, the mother does not learn to love, but kills even her own child to solve her problems. And, by abortion, the father is told that he does not have to take any responsibility at all for the child he has brought into the world. That father is likely to put other women into the same trouble. So abortion just leads to more abortion. Any country that accepts abortion is not teaching its people to love, but to use any violence to get what they want. This is why the greatest destroyer of love and peace is abortion.

Many people are very, very concerned with the children of India, with the children of Africa where quite a few die of hunger, and so on. Many people are also concerned about all the violence in this great country of the United States. These concerns are very good. But often these same people are not concerned with the millions who are being killed by the deliberate decision of their own mothers. And this is what is the greatest destroyer of peace today - abortion which brings people to such blindness.

And for this I appeal in India and I appeal everywhere – "Let us bring the child back." The child is God's gift to the family. Each child is created in the special image and likeness of God for greater things - to love and to be loved. In this year of the family we must bring the child back to the center of our care and concern. This is the only

way that our world can survive because our children are the only hope for the future. As older people are called to God, only their children are can take their places.

But what does God say to us? He says: "Even if a mother could forget her child, I will not forget you. I have carved you in the palm of my hand." We are carved in the palm of His hand; that unborn child has been carved in the hand of God from conception and is called by God to love and to be loved, not only now in this life, but forever. God can never forget us.

I will tell you something beautiful. We are fighting abortion by adoption - by care of the mother and adoption for her baby. We have saved thousands of lives. We have sent word to the clinics, to the hospitals and police stations: "Please don't destroy the child; we will take the child." So we always have someone tell the mothers in trouble: "Come, we will take care of you, we will get a home for your child." And we have a tremendous demand from couples who cannot have a child - but I never give a child to a couple who have done something not to have a child. Jesus said, "Anyone who receives a child in my name, receives me." By adopting a child, these couples receive Jesus but, by aborting a child, a couple refuses to receive Jesus.

Please don't kill the child. I want the child. Please give me the child. I am willing to accept any child who would be aborted and to give that child to a married couple who will love the child and be loved by the child. From our children's home in Calcutta alone, we have saved over 3000 children from abortion. These children have brought such love and joy to their adopting parents and have grown up so full of love and joy.

I know that couples have to plan their family and for that there is natural family planning. In destroying the power of giving life, through contraception, a husband or wife is doing something to self. This turns the attention to self and so it destroys the gift of love in him or her. In loving, the husband and wife must turn the attention to each other as happens in natural family planning, and not to self, as happens in contraception . Once that living love is destroyed by contraception, abortion follows very easily.

I also know that there are great problems in the world - that many spouses do not love each other enough to practice natural family planning.

We cannot solve all the problems in the world, but let us never bring in the worst problem of all, and that is to destroy love. And this is what happens when we tell people to practice contraception and abortion.

The poor are very great people. They can teach us so many beautiful things. Once one of them came to thank us for teaching her natural family planning and said: "You people who have practiced chastity, you are the best people to teach us natural family planning because it is nothing more than self-control out of love for each other." And what this poor person said is very true. These poor people maybe have nothing to eat, maybe they have not a home to live in, but they can still be great people when they are spiritually rich.

When I pick up a person from the street, hungry, I give him a plate of rice, a piece of bread. But a person who is shut out, who feels unwanted, unloved, terrified, the person who has been thrown out of society - that spiritual poverty is much harder to overcome. And abortion, which often follows from contraception, brings a people to be spiritually poor, and that is the worst poverty and the most difficult to overcome.

Those who are materially poor can be very wonderful people. One evening we went out and we picked up four people from the street. And one of them was in a most terrible condition. I told the Sisters: "You take care of the other three; I will take care of the one who looks worse." So I did for her all that my love can do. I put her in bed, and there was such a beautiful smile on her face, She took hold of my hand, as she said one word only: "thank you" - and she died.

I could not help but examine my conscience before her. And I said: "What would I say if I were in her place?" And my answer was very simple. I would have tried to draw a little attention to myself. I would have said: "I am hungry, I am dying, I am cold, I am in pain," or something. But she gave me much more - she gave me her grateful love. And she died with a smile on her face. Then there was the man we picked up from the drain, half eaten by worms and, after we had brought him to the home, he only said, "I have lived like an animal in the street, but I am going to die as an angel, loved and cared for." Then, after we had removed all the worms from his body, all he said, with a big smile, was: "Sister, I am going home to God" -and he died. It was so wonderful to see the greatness of that man who could speak like that without blaming anybody, without comparing anything. Like and angel - this is the greatness of people who are spiritually rich even when they are materially poor.

We are not social workers. We may be doing social work in the eyes of some people, but we must be contemplatives in the heart of the world. For we must bring that presence of God into your family, for the family that prays together, stays together. There is so much hatred, so much misery, and we with our prayer, with our sacrifice, are beginning at home. Love begins at home, and it is not how much we do, but how much love we put into what we do.

If we are contemplatives in the heart of the world with all its problems, these problems can never discourage us. We must always remember what God tells us in Scripture: "Even if a mother could forget the child in her womb - something-impossible but even if she could forget - I will never forget you.

And so here I am talking with you. I want you to find the poor here, right in your own home first. And begin love there. Bring that good news to your own people first. And find out about your next-door neighbors. Do you know who they are?

I had the most extraordinary experience of love of neighbor with a Hindu family. A gentleman came to our house and said: "Mother Teresa, there is a family who have not eaten for so long. Do something." So I took some rice and went there immediately. And I saw the children - their eyes shining with hunger. I don't know if you have ever seen hunger. But I have seen it very often. And the mother of the family took the rice I gave her and went out. When she came back, I asked her: "Where did you go? What did you do?" And she gave me a very simple answer: "They are hungry also." What struck me was that she knew - and who are they? A Muslim family - and she knew. I didn't bring any more rice that evening because I wanted them, Hindus and Muslims, to enjoy the joy of sharing.

But there were those children, radiating joy, sharing the joy and peace with their mother because she had the love to give until it hurts. And you see this is where love begins - at home in the family.

So, as the example of this family shows, God will never forget us and there is something you and

I can always do. We can keep the joy of loving Jesus in our hearts, and share that joy with all we come in contact with. Let us make that one point - that no child will be unwanted, unloved, uncared for, or killed and thrown away. And give until it hurts - with a smile.

Because I talk so much of giving with a smile, once a professor from the United States asked me: "Are you married?" And I said: "Yes, and I find it sometimes very difficult to smile at my spouse, Jesus, because He can be very demanding - sometimes." This is really something true. And there is where love comes in - when it is demanding, and yet we can give it with joy.

One of the most demanding things for me is travelling everywhere - and with publicity. I have said to Jesus that if I don't go to heaven for anything else, I will be going to heaven for all the travelling with all the publicity, because it has purified me and sanctified me and made me really ready to go to heaven.

If we remember that God loves us, and that we can love others as He loves us, then America can become a sign of peace for the world. From here, a sign of care for the weakest of the weak - the unborn child - must go out to the world. If you become a burning light of justice and peace in the world, then really you will be true to what the founders of this country stood for. God bless you!

History of America's Education

Providence Foundation

History of America's Education

In the 1980s The National Commission on Excellence in Education issued a report entitled "A Nation at Risk." In that report they stated: "If *an unfriendly foreign power had attempted to impose on America the mediocre educational performance that exists today, we might well have viewed it as an act of war.*"

Why are we a nation at risk today? One primary reason is due to the mediocre educational performance that exists today that results from the state monopoly of education where the anti-Christian, man-centered religion of humanism is preached 5 days a week to 40-50 million of our youth, which is leading them and our nation into bondage.

This man-is-god religion (where man is the source of right and wrong and there are no absolutes) is also predominant in the market place of ideas——In the media, movies, television, and arts.

Johnny is in trouble today.

Johnny is in trouble – not because he is playing hooky from school, but because he is attending school.

Some of the most negative influences that young Americans can face today are found in public schools. In the past few decades this has exponentially worsened. In 1940 the top offenses in public schools were chewing gum, talking in class, unfinished homework, and running in the halls. In 1980 the top offenses were drugs, drunkenness, assault, murder and rape.

While at school, Johnny not only is confronted with drugs, immorality and violence, but he is also receiving a second rate education. From 1963 - 1980 Scholastic Aptitude Test scores dropped consistently each year (since 1980 they increased slightly for a few years and then began dropping again). The average verbal scores of the SAT dropped over 50 points and the average math scores dropped over 35 points.

As a result of decreasing literary skills, college textbooks are being rewritten at a lower grade level so that the students can understand them. Most newspapers and magazines are written at about a sixth grade level which is now the reading level of the average American. [To compare the literacy level of today with early America, read the *Federalist Papers,* which were written for farmers and other common citizens in New York. Today's college graduates find them difficult.]

"But how can this be?" you may ask, "for Johnny is getting better grades than ever." This is true, which makes the problem even worse, for many young people do not know how little they are learning.

Take for example, the young man who graduated as valedictorian from his Washington, D.C. high school yet was refused admission to George Washington University because his SAT scores were so low (320 on the verbal, which was the bottom 13% nationally of high school seniors; and 280 on the math, which was the bottom 2%). Due to his excellent grades he understandably considered himself a superior student, yet in the words of the dean of admissions of George Washington University, "He's been deluded into thinking he's gotten an education."

He, like many others in our public education system, has been conned. Grade inflation has only contributed to hiding the crisis that faces our public schools today.

Many Americans have been deluded into thinking they have gotten an education. They may not be functionally illiterate (though tens of millions are), but way too many are culturally and morally illiterate.

What is the problem?

Educational leaders acknowledge that there are problems with our public schools. Most of their suggested solutions involve spending more money (or in centralizing education). In the past few decades, however, the public education system has dramatically increased its expenditures – in 1950 $8.8 billion was spent on education in America; in 1985, $261 billion; in 1990, $353 billion; and in 1992, $445 billion. Elementary and high schools spent $274 billion in 1992-93. After adjusting for inflation, spending was up 40% in the 10 years since 1982-1983. Well over $5000 per student per year is spent (on the average) in secondary public education. [Washington D.C. schools spend almost $10,000 per child, but is near the bottom of all cities nationally in academics.] Yet with all this spending, the educational skills of our students have decreased.

Lack of money is not the problem in our public schools. The problems have not been due to a lack of financial resources, but of spiritual resources. The problem is with the philosophy that forms the foundation of education in America. **Colossians 2:8** is very insightful in this matter:

"See to it that no one takes you captive through philosophy and empty deception, according to the tradition of men, according to the elementary principles of the world, rather than according to Christ."

There are two basic philosophies – that which is according to the world, and that which is according to Christ. A worldly or humanistic (man-centered) philosophy always brings captivity or bondage, while a Christian philosophy brings liberty.

A worldly educational philosophy has controlled our public schools for some time. The result is bondage. For example, there are at least 40 million American adults who are functionally illiterate – they cannot read a want ad, a job application form, a label on a medicine bottle, or a safety sign at a work place. That is bondage! A vast majority of these people went to school enough to supposedly learn how to read. A more recent study has shown that 90 million American adults are unable to function in society due to lack of basic educational skills.

It has been said that **the philosophy of education in one generation will be the philosophy of government in the next.** The direction our nation has been going in recent decades is a result of the training those governing America have received in the schools in the past. Noah Webster knew the importance of educating youth.

Webster has been called the father of American scholarship and education. He affected the course of education in early America more than any other person. His blue-backed speller sold over 100 million copies from 1783 through the 1800s, and was designed to allow individuals to be self-taught. Webster spent over 26 years working on his dictionary, the first exhaustive dictionary of the English language. He was the first person to do extensive etymological research, mastering 28 languages during this study and writing of the dictionary. Besides his speller, he wrote a grammar, a reader, a U.S. History, and other textbooks. He translated his own version of the Bible, helped to start a college, started the first magazine in America, and started a newspaper. He was one of the first persons to publicly promote a constitutional convention in the 1780s. He secured copyright legislation on the state and national levels, served in civil government in many capacities, and wrote on a wide variety of topics. During his astoundingly productive life he also lovingly raised seven children. We would do well to listen to him.

Noah Webster wrote in the March, 1788, American Magazine: *"the education of youth [is] an employment of more consequence than making laws and preaching the gospel, because it lays the foundation on which both law and gospel rest for success."*

Is this true or heresy? It depends upon how you define education. It is certainly not true based upon modern views of education. *Webster's New World Dictionary of the American Language* defines education as:

"1. the process of educating especially by formal schooling; teaching; training. 2. knowledge, ability, etc. thus developed. 3. a) formal schooling. b) a kind or stage of this: as, a medical education. 4. systematic study of the methods and theories of teaching and learning."

However, if we looked at how Webster defined education in his original dictionary published in 1828, we would readily agree with his statement. In this dictionary, Webster defined words biblically and generously used scriptural references. [Webster wouldn't recognize the dictionary that bears his name today.] His definition was:

"Education - The bringing up, as a child,, instruction; formation of manners. Education comprehends all that series of instruction and discipline which is intended to enlighten the understanding, correct the temper, and form the manners and habits of youth, and fit them for usefulness in their future stations. To give children a good education in manners, arts and science, is important; to give them a religious education is indispensable; and an immense responsibility rests on parents and guardians who neglect these duties."

To Webster, the central goal of education was to train youth in the precepts of Christianity. He stated, "*In my view, the Christian religion is the most important and one of the first things in which all children, under a free government, ought to be instructed... No truth is more evident to my mind than that the Christian religion must be the basis of any government intended to secure the rights and privileges of a free people.*"

We can see why such education lays the foundation for the success of the Gospel and the making of good laws, for only a people of good character and ideas can preserve religious and civil liberty. It was such a people that gave birth to liberty throughout the world. In Webster's *United States History* book, he has a chapter on the U.S. Constitution. In there is a section with the heading, *Origin of Civil Liberty,* which contains this:

"*Almost all the civil liberty now enjoyed in the world owes its origin to the principles of the Christian religion... The religion which has introduced civil liberty, is the religion of Christ and his apostles, which enjoins humility, piety, and benevolence; which acknowledges in every person a brother, or a sister, and a citizen with equal rights. This is genuine Christianity, and to this we owe our free constitutions of government...* "

How we educate the next generation will determine how our nation is governed in the next generation. This is why education of youth is of utmost importance.

Education in Early America

Education in early America was much different than that of today, in form and results. Most education was done by the home or church. This is where the ideas and character were implanted in our founders. Such training produced one of the greatest group of men – in thought and character – of all time.

Samuel Blumenfeld says: "*Of the 117 men who signed the Declaration of Independence, the Articles of Confederation and the Constitution, one out of three had had only a few months of formal schooling, and only one in four had gone to college. They were educated by parents, church schools, tutors, academies, apprenticeship, and by themselves.*"

They were a product of a system of education much different than today.

What was education in early America like?

1. Education was centered in the home.

Almost every child in America was educated. At the time of the Revolution, the literacy level was virtually 100% (even on the frontier it was greater than 70 %). John Adams said to find someone who couldn't read was as rare as a comet. The colonists had a Christian philosophy of education – they felt everyone should be educated, because everyone needed to know the truth for themselves.

Tutors were at times hired to supplement education. Ministers were most often the tutors. Many of the founders of America had ministers as tutors including Jefferson, Madison, and Noah Webster. Those that went to colleges would have been instructed by ministers.

2. First schools were started by the church.

The first school in New England was the Boston Latin School. It was started in 1636 by Rev.

John Cotton to provide education for those who were not able to receive it at home.

For centuries, most schools were Church schools, started by the major Christian sects. Some of these schools charged moderate tuition fees, but generally taught the children of the poor for free.

3. First common (public) schools were thoroughly Christian.

Massachusetts Education Laws:
• In 1642 the General Court enacted legislation requiring each town to see that children were taught, especially *"to read and understand the principles of religion and the capital laws of this country..."*
• The "Old Deluder Satan" Act of 1647 stated: *"It being one chief project of that old deluder, Satan, to keep men from the knowledge of the Scriptures..."* The General Court went on to order any town with 50 families to hire a teacher, and those that increased to 100 families to set up a school to prepare youth for the university.

Grammar School at Dorchester, MA: Rules adopted by town meeting in 1645 required the schoolmaster *"to commend his scholars and his labors amongst them unto God by prayer morning and evening, taking care that his scholars do reverently attend during the same."* The schoolmaster examined each student at noon on Monday to see what he had learned from the Sabbath sermon. On Friday afternoon at 2:00, he was to catechize them *"in the principles of Christian religion."*

As time went on private schools flourished more than common schools (especially as the Puritan influence in common schools decreased). The Christian community saw the private schools were more reliable. *"By 1720 Boston had far more private schools than public ones, and by the close of the American Revolution many towns had no common schools... at all."*

Most of the schools in the Middle and Southern Colonies were church schools. Public schools in the Middle Colonies were found only in the cities, and they were still in a minority. There were no public schools in the Southern colonies until 1730 and only five by 1776. Remember, the colonies has a literacy level (both quantity and quality) equal to or greater than that of today with our tens of thousands of schools and hundreds of billions of dollars supporting state education.

4. Character of teachers

To reveal the character of the teachers in early America many examples could be given, from Ezekiel Cheever (1614-1708) a schoolmaster for 70 years in New England, to Noah Webster, Emma Willard, and many ministers. We will briefly examine one, **Nathan Hale.**

Hale taught school in East Haddarn, Connecticut after he graduated from Yale College in the fall of 1773 at age 18. After 4 or 5 months at this country schoolhouse, he accepted the position of mastership of a private school in New London. He wrote to friends: "I love my employment." In July, 1775 he resigned to accept a commission in the Colonial Army.

During the early, years of the Revolutionary War, information of the position and strength of the British troops was vitally needed by the American forces. Someone was needed to disguise themselves and travel behind the enemy lines to attempt to obtain this data. Captain Nathan Hale volunteered for this hazardous service because he saw it as an opportunity to serve his country and further the cause of liberty.

Disguised as a civilian, Hale passed into Long Island and observed the position, strength, and movement of the British army. As he was attempting to return, he was captured, carried before Sir William Howe, where he confessed his rank in the American army and his purpose, which the papers he was carrying confirmed. Orders were immediately given for Hale to be executed the next morning as a spy.

One historian writes: *"The order was accordingly executed in a most unfeeling manner, and by as great a savage as ever disgraced humanity. A clergyman, whose attendance he desired, was refused him; a bible for a moment's devotion was not procured, though he requested it. Letters, which on the morning of his execution, he wrote to his mother, and other friends, were destroyed, and this very extraordinary reason given by the provost marshal, 'that the rebels should not know that they had a man in their army, who could die with so much firmness.'*

Unknown to those around him, and without a single friend to offer him the least consolation, Hale ascended the gallows on the morning of September 22, 1776, offering these words as his dying observation: *"I only regret that I have but one life to lose for my country."*

This courageous young man saw the value of liberty, and was motivated by its light. *"Neither expectation of promotion nor pecuniary reward, induced him to this attempt. A sense of duty, a hope that he might in this way be useful to his country, and an opinion which he had adopted, that every kind of service necessary to the public good, became honourable by being necessary, were the great motives which induced him to engage in an enterprise by which his connections lost a most amiable friend, and his country one of its most promising supporters."*

This is the type of character teachers in early America possessed. This same type of character is needed by teachers today. Teachers today may not have to physically give up their life for the cause of liberty, but they should inspire those they teach to see the necessity of doing all they can to preserve our God given liberty and rights.

5. Apprenticeship or college

Up until age 8, almost all colonial youth were taught at home. At around this age, some had tutors to supplement their education and some attended schools. At around age 13-15, the young men would be apprenticed at some trade (often at home) or some few would attend college.

6. Colleges and Universities

106 of the first 108 colleges were started on the Christian faith. By the close of 1860 there were 246 colleges in America. Seventeen of these were state institutions; almost every other one was founded by Christian denominations or by individuals who avowed a religious purpose. Many of the state colleges were Christian as well.

Harvard College, 1636

The following report on Harvard College, from "New Englands First Fruits" published in 1643, reveals the purpose for it's establishment:

"After God had carried us safe to New England, and wee had builded our houses, provided necessaries for our liveli-hood, rear'd convenient places for Gods worship, and settled the Civil Government: One of the next things we longed for, and looked after was to advance Learning, and perpetuate it to Posterity, dreading to leave an illiterate Ministry to the Churches, when our present Ministers shall lie in the Dust."

An Original Rule of Harvard College:

"Let every Student be plainly instructed, and earnestly pressed to consider well, the maine end of his life and studies is, to know God and Jesus Christ which is eternall life, (John 17:3), and therefore to lay Christ in the bottom, as the only foundation of all sound knowledge and learning."

William and Mary, 1691

The College of William and Mary was started mainly due to the efforts of Rev. James Blair in order, according to its charter of 1691, *"that the Church of Virginia may be furnished with a seminary of ministers of the Gospel, and that the youth may be piously educated in good letters and manners, and that the Christian religion may be propagated among the Western Indians to the glory of Almighty God."*

Yale University, 1701

Yale University was started by Congregational ministers in 1701, *"for the liberal and religious education of suitable youth... to propagate in this wilderness, the blessed reformed Protestant religion..."*

Princeton, 1746

Associated with the Great Awakening, Princeton was founded by the Presbyterians in 1746. Rev. Jonathan Dickinson became its first president, declaring, *"cursed be all that learning that is contrary to the cross of Christ"* To help raise funds for the college in England, a General Account was prepared that stated *"the two principal Objects the Trustees had in View, were Science and Religion. Their first Concern was to cultivate the Minds of the Pupils, in all those Branches of Erudition, which are generally taught in the Universities abroad; and to perfect their Design, their next Care was to rectify the Heart, by inculcating the great Precepts of Christianity, in order to make them good men"*

University of Pennsylvania, 1751

Ben Franklin had much to do with the beginning of the University of Pennsylvania. It was not started by a denomination, but its laws reflect its Christian character. Consider the first two *Laws, relating to the Moral Conduct, and Orderly Behaviour, of the Students and Scholars of the University of Pennsylvania* (from 1801):

"1. None of the students or scholars, belonging to this seminary, shall make use of any indecent or immoral language: whether it consist in immodest expressions; in cursing and swearing; or in exclamations which introduce the name of GOD, without reverence, and without necessity.

"2. None of them shall, without a good and sufficient reason, be absent from school, or late in his attendance; more particularly at the time of prayers, and of the reading of the Holy Scriptures."

Columbia, 1754

In 1754, Samuel Johnson became the first president of Columbia (called King's College up until 1784). In that year he composed an advertisement announcing the opening of the college. It stated:

"The chief Thing that is aimed at in this College is, to teach and engage the Children to know God in Jesus Christ, and to love and serve him, in all Sobriety, Godliness and Righteousness of Life, with a perfect Heart, and a willing Mind; and to train them up in all virtuous Habits, and all such useful Knowledge as may render them creditable to their Families and Friends..."

Dartmouth, 1770

Congregational pastor Eleazar Wheelock (1711-79) secured a charter from the governor of New Hampshire in March, 1770, to establish a college to train young men for missionary service among the Indians. The college was named after Lord Dartmouth of England who assisted in raising funds for its establishment. Its Latin motto means: *"the voice of one crying in the wilderness."* The first students met in a log cabin and when weather permitted Dr. Wheelock held morning and evening prayers in the open air.

Some other colleges started before America's Independence include: Brown, started by the Baptists in 1764; Rutgers, 1766, by the Dutch Reformed Church; Washington and Lee, 1749; and Hampden-Sidney, 1776, by the Presbyterians.

7. Textbooks

The Bible and its principles were the focal point of education. In 1690, John Locke said that children learned to read by following *"the ordinary road of Hornbook, Primer, Psalter, Testament and Bible."*

The New Haven Code of 1655 required that children be made *"able duly to read the Scriptures... and in some competent measure to understand the main grounds and principles of Christian Religion necessary to salvation."*

a. The **Bible** was the central text

John Adams reflected the view of the founders in regard to the place of the Bible in society when he wrote:

"Suppose a nation in some distant Region, should take the Bible for their only law-book, and every member should regulate his conduct by the precepts there exhibited!... What a Utopia; what a Paradise would this region be!" John Adams, Feb. 22, 1756.

b. Hornbooks

Hornbooks had been used to teach children to read from as far back as 1400 in Europe. They came to America with the colonists and were common from the 1500s - 1700s. A hornbook was a flat piece of wood with a handle, upon which a sheet of printed paper was attached and covered with transparent animal horn to protect it. A typical hornbook had the alphabet, the vowels, a list of syllables, the invocation of the Trinity, and the Lord's Prayer. Some had a pictured alphabet.

c. Catechisms

Catechisms were used extensively in early education in America. There were over 500 different catechisms according to Increase Mather. The most widely used catechism was one which the Puritans brought with them from England, *The Foundation of Christian Religion gathered into sixe, Principles,* by William Perkins. Later, the Westminster Catechism became the most prominent one.

d. The New England Primer

Another important educational book was the New England Primer, which was first published in Boston around 1690 by devote Protestant Benjamin Harris. It was the most prominent schoolbook for about 100 years, and was frequently reprinted through the 1800s. It sold over 3 million copies in 150 years. The rhyming alphabet is its most characteristic feature.

From a 1777 Primer, the alphabet was taught with this rhyme:

A   In Adam's Fall
     We sinned all.
B   Heaven to find
     The Bible Mind.
C   Christ crucify'd
     For sinners dy'd.
D   The Deluge drown'd
     The Earth around.
E   Elijah hid
     By Ravens fed.
F   The judgment made
     Felix afraid.
G   As runs the Glass,
     Our Life doth pass
H   My Book and Heart
     Must never part ....

It is easy to see its Christian character. The Primer underwent various modifications over the years.

e.   Webster's Blue-Backed Speller

Webster's speller was first published in 1783 and sold over 100 million copies during the next century. It was the most influential textbook of the era and was written to instill into the minds of the youth "the first rudiments of the language and some just ideas of religion, morals, and domestic economy." Its premise was that "God's word, contained in the Bible, has furnished all necessary rules to direct our conduct." It included a moral catechism, large portions of the Sermon on the Mount, a paraphrase of the Genesis account of creation, and numerous moral stories.

f.   The McGuffey Readers

Written by minister and university professor William Holmes McGuffey, the *McGuffey Readers* "represent the most significant force in the framing of our national morals and tastes" other than the Bible. First published in 1836, they sold over 122 million copies in 75 years and are still used today in some schools. McGuffey wrote in the Preface to the Fourth Reader:

"From no source has the author drawn more copiously, in his selections, than from the sacred Scriptures. For this, he certainly apprehends no censure. In a Christian country, that man is to be pitied, who at this day, can honestly object to imbuing the minds of youth with the language and spirit of the Word of God."

While there were many other textbooks (especially in the 1800s), the ones just mentioned were some of the most important.

Education in Religion was central to our Founders

We have already given quotes of Noah Webster, Samuel Adams, John Adams, Franklin, Penn, and Daniel Webster, and could talk quite sometime of the Biblical view America's founders had of education. We will look at only a few more comments.

Benjamin Rush was a signer of the Declaration of Independence; a professor of medicine, making many contributions in that field in practice and writing; a leader in societies for the abolition of slavery; president of various Bible and medical societies; a principal founder of Dickenson College; and a leader in education. Concerning education he wrote:

"I proceed, in the next place, to enquire what mode of education we shall adopt so as to secure to the state all the advantages that are to be derived from the proper instruction of youth; and here I beg leave to remark that the only foundation for a useful education in a republic is to be laid in religion. Without this, there can be no virtue, and without virtue there can be no liberty, and liberty is the object and life of all republican governments."

Gouverneur Morris, a signer of the Constitution, wrote: *"Religion is the only solid basis of good morals; therefore, education should teach the precepts of religion, and the duties of man towards God."*

Fisher Ames said *"the Bible [should] retain the place it once held as a school book. Its morals are pure, its examples captivating and noble. The reverence for the sacred book that is thus early impressed lasts long; and probably, if not impressed in infancy, never takes firm hold of the mind."*

Northwest Ordinance, 1787 (1789): *"Religion, morality and knowledge, being necessary to good government and the happiness of mankind, schools and the means of education shall forever be encouraged."*

The type of education that shaped our Founders character and ideas was thoroughly Christian. It imparted Christian character and produced honest, industrious, compassionate, respectful, and law-abiding men. It also imparted a Biblical world-view and produced people who were principled thinkers.

This was reflected in the constitutions and laws of our states and nation. America was established as the first constitutional federal republic in history. Christian principles of self-government, union, virtue, the value of the individual, and recognition of God-given inalienable rights to life, liberty and property are incorporated in our nation's fabric. Christian economic principles of individual enterprise, private property rights, and the free market formed the foundation of our prosperity as a nation.

In early America, the people made the laws and the churches made the people. Their ideas and character were shaped by Christianity.

Printed by permission from the Providence Foundation
PO Box 6759, Charlottesville, Virginia 22906

The Sins of Compromise

Plymouth Rock Foundation

A publication of The Plymouth Rock Foundation, Marlborough, NH 03455

THE SINS OF COMPROMISE*

Enter ye in at the strait gate: for wide is the gate, and broad is the way, that leadeth to destruction, and many there be which go in there at. Because strait is the gate, and narrow is the way, which leadeth unto life, and few there are that find it." Matthew 7:13,14

When you get right down to it, there are just two ways to go. Just two.

And each of us must choose: One, or the other. What will it be?

The choice we make, determines our condition both here and in eternity.

There is the right way. And the wrong. The good way, and the evil.

There is the path to life. And, the road to death.

The road to death and destruction is broad.

It may be paved with good intentions but more often than not it is surfaced with wicked desire and evil design. It twists and turns and adapts to every expediency; it configures to all manner of devilish propositions.

It is the road of the prince of darkness; it is the way of the multitudes.

Through its wide and many-splendored facades, the individual may enter with all his excess baggage; all his appetites and ego and vanities intact; all his graven images and idols in tow. To coin a phrase: This road is "hell-bent" for destruction—and death.

There is another road!

This road is narrow. It is hedged on both sides by unyielding demands and specific commands. It does not twist; it does not turn. It acknowledges no expediencies, seeks no compromise, brooks no concessions.

It is the way of "the little flock."

To gain access to this narrow road one must first seek and find the straight and narrow gate. Those who find it, those who are called to enter, must deny self, must cast aside all desire for the things of this world. Yet, even then, only Divine Grace holds the key which opens this gate; for no man is worthy.

Only the atoning blood of Jesus Christ, the only begotten Son of God, The Savior, makes possible that which, for the individual, is impossible.

Any suggestion that once a person passes through the strait gate the way becomes smooth and easy would be a gross deception (Mt 10:34-39). There is great joy, yes! And many blessings, too! But, those who are called must not only cast aside the things of this world while going forth into the world; they must take up the cross of Christ and follow Him. They must stand with Him, stand for Him ... and proclaim Him.

The Savior who died that we might have life is also Our King. Him only are we to serve. Serving Him by being obediently faithful to Him. And often serving Him by serving others in His precious name.

Between the two, between the road to destruction and the way of light and life—there is no middle ground.

For, the master of each road wages war continuously – all – out – war against the other. Thus, for The Master's soldiers there can be no compromise. Never.

Our Savior and our King has made that abundantly and irrevocably clear. In His purity and His truth, He has set the example which His must strive to follow.

Consider, for instance, how He was tempted by satan after forty days and nights of fasting in the in the wilderness (Mt 4:1-11). Think about that ultimate temptation, there on that exceeding high mountain with all the kingdoms of the world spread out before Him.

"All these things will I give you," bargained satan, *"if you will fall down and worship me."*

"Get thee hence," rebuked The Christ, *"for it is written, Thou shalt worship The Lord thy God, and Him only shalt thou serve."*

Christ entertained no thought of compromise. No concession. No bargaining. Not then. Not ever. And so it must be also for those who would follow Him. He tells us so. Here, hear His word:

"Whosoever shall confess Me before men, him will I confess also before My Father which is in heaven. But, whosoever deny me before men, him will I also deny before My Father which is in heaven"

"No man can serve two masters," warned Jesus, "for *either he will hate the one and love the other; or else he will hold to the one and despise the other. You cannot serve God and mammon"* (Mt 6:24).

Nor can you be lukewarm. His warning is clear: *"For, if you are, I will spew thee out of My mouth"* (Rev 3:16).

What Christ said to those of the church at Laodicea, He says also to us. Now. In this day.

And then there was Paul! Paul who had been Saul. He knew all about the sins of compromise.

Before God had struck him down and raised him up, Paul had been party to the persecution of the Christians who had refused to compromise. He knew the price they had paid, the pain they had endured, the way they had died. Yet, after his conversion, did Paul urge believers to concede, to yield, to compromise, so that they might escape the stones of the mob and the wrath of the authorities? He did not!

"Stand fast," urged Paul. *"Contend for the faith,"* he pleaded. *"Fight the good fight!"*

Have no fellowship with the unrighteous. That's what Paul said!

Have no communion with darkness. No concord with infidels. No covenant with the ungodly.

You are the temple of The Living God; what agreement has the temple of God with idols? Has not God said, *"Come out from among them and be you separate?"* (2 Cor 16:14-18).

What could be more clear? More direct? More specific?

Have no fellowship with the unrighteous. Make no pacts.

Seek no compromises; accept none. You have been bought with a price! You are not your own.

Have no part of any unclean things.

"Let us hear the conclusion of the whole matter: Fear God and keep His commandments: for this is the whole duty of man. For God shall bring every work into judgment, with every secret thing, whether it be good, or whether it be evil" (Ecc 11: 13,14).

Yet, there are those, even those who profess to believe on His name, who counsel Christians to be more flexible; less rigid.

Those who advise us that the way to get along in this world is to go along with some of the ways of the world. Not all things, mind you; not all the time; just now and then—when it is expedient, when it "is necessary."

Paul's admonitions not withstanding, Christ's commandments to the contrary, they assure us there can be common cause with darkness.

Examine a few of their suggestions; consider some of the compromises they would have us make:

- to appear less rigid and more flexible, go along with abortion, at least in the first trimester,

- to protect the right to operate our Christian schools, go along with State standards. Sure, they're a little humanistic and ungodly—but perhaps we'll get a tax write-off, and right now it's tough to operate our "Christian" schools.

- (Well, that which Caesar funds, Caesar controls. How can we invite Caesar to control that which bears the name or, and pledges fidelity to, Jesus Christ? Such an institution is no school for Jesus and no school for the followers of Christ. It is, indeed a wolf in disguise, waiting to divert and devour the little children of His flock!!)

- to maintain our freedom of worship and the tax exempt status of the church we should avoid any active interest in civil affairs ("After all, we must obey the magistrates, and besides, what about separation of church and State!").

- to be more effective in the public forum, we're told to moderate our stand against euthanasia and other anti-life proposals and not be so dogmatic on other Biblical principles and precepts morality, on godliness and right conduct (after all, who are we to judge?)

- to show Christian tolerance, we should drop (or, at least, soften) our opposition to subsidizing the fraud of evolution in our public schools;
- to be less anti-social, we should stop insisting that the State stop intruding upon family affairs and cease and desist infringing on parental rights and responsibilities.

"Yeah, hath God said?" Has He given such instruction to His followers? Are we truly to cut our faith and bend our standards to make peace with a wicked world? Where? Where does He say we should turn our back on Him and His commandments to gain smiles from the lost and depraved?

Mark the words in His Holy Scriptures. Check His demands in both the Old and the New Covenants. Those pacts He has made with those who are truly His.

"Thou shalt have no other gods before Me."
"If you love Me, keep My commandments."

His word stands. Immutable, in errant, unchanging and forever. I shall not pass away. Tamper with it, twist it, modify it at your risk!

Those who would have us reject the totality and truth of God's word would also have us accept a watered down, revised, bent and twisted history of the Christ's church ... Christ's true church. Not a feel-good status with its influence measured by the heighth of its steeple, the size of its spa and the length of it's limousines.

Those who would have us get along by going along would have us believe that Christianity made its greatest progress and had its greatest impact when it was "flexible," when it was "moderate," when it compromised its stand and muted Bible truths, played to the crowd and straddled the line between God and mammon.

They ignore the facts. The opposite is true.

It was, for example, when the church made common cause and compromise with Constantine that the curse of God befell it. It was then that delusion, idolatry and paganism, crept into and became a part of that institution.

It was when the Church of England sought power through compromise with earthly kings rather than obedience to Him that God brought spiritual sickness upon it; a pernicious slumber that persisted until the likes of Wycliffe and

Tyndale, Calvin and Wesley and Whitefield came forth to shake it loose from the bondage and paralysis of heresy and apostasy.

And, it was when Christianity in America compromised with humanism and modernity that it began to lose its influence in the land. Who, then, could honestly be surprised when paganism has infested our schools, our civil institutions, our arts and sciences, our houses of commerce... and, our churches?

Here is fact:

When an uncompromising, intolerant, inhospitable Christianity refused to yield to the demands of the world, when it refused to modify its faith or bend a single knee or stretch a single principle, when it stood firmly on The Rock and brooked no twist or turn in Truth — it was then it had its greatest impact and made its most dynamic growth.

And it was then that it spread its most benevolent effects. For, it was then that it had the blessing of The Lord God Jehovah and the power of The Holy Ghost.

Consider those days of the apostles! Never did The Gospel make more progress or produce more glorious results. Yet, never did Christianity face greater obstacles. Imagine: *twelve against the world!* Surely, if there were ever a time for compromise, for concession, for moderation, that was it. But, this the apostles knew and this we also must recognize:

The world is not won by giving ground; the victory is gained by standing ground and drawing the world unto Jesus Christ!

What would have happened to Christianity if the apostles had caved in? Where would it be today if it had not been for the inspired inflexibility of Luther, the perseverance of Huss, the determination of Calvin that laid the foundations for a new nation, the persistence of Knox that rescued Protestantism in Scotland?

Or, the obstinance of the Lollards, the determination of the Separatists, the devotion of the Pilgrims, and the convictions of the Baptists? And the Presbyterians. These, too, like the apostles at the start, were used of God to turn the world around, to lead the way to repentance and revival and reformation—and to move the chain of Christianity westward to these shores and then throughout the world!

As followers of Jesus Christ, the Living,

141

reigning King, we are to strive to be His living examples. Society does, in fact, judge a faith by those who profess to be faithful. Thus:

If the Word of God is truly truth... <u>and indeed He is!</u>

If Biblical principles and precepts have any definite meaning and certain application ... and <u>indeed they do.</u>

If God does command any specific rudiments of life, any definite attributes of Christian character, any inflexible code of conduct, and <u>He does for sure!</u>

And, if He does fix certain bounds and boundaries within which the Christian life is circumscribed and separated from the world ...

... then those are the things that cannot be compromised, those are the command-ments that must be obeyed; those are the principles by which we must govern ourselves.

From that moment when we accept Christ as Savior and make Him our King, we are to embark upon an unyielding, uncompromising way of life. It may seem intolerant to some and inhospitable to others. But, remember always the words of the apostles as they stood before the magistrates:

"Whether it be right in the sight of God to hearken unto men more than unto God, judge ye"

———————

Printed by permission from the Plymouth Rock Foundation
Fisk Mill, PO Box 425, Marlborough, New Hampshire 03455

The Lampstand:

Is It Leaving America

Mario Murillo

The Lampstand: Is It Leaving America

by Mario Murillo -from FreshFire Times, January, 1997
Mario Murillo Ministries, 425 El Pintado Rd., Danville, CA 94526

Dear Friend,

As I am writing to you, a frightening evaluation is going on in Heaven. Let me tell you what it is. God is about to decide if America should keep her lampstand as the seat of the Christian faith. Look with me at the Book of Revelation:

"The mystery of the seven stars which you saw, in My right hand, and the seven golden lampstands: The seven stars are the angels of the seven churches, and the seven lampstands which you saw are the seven churches. " (Rev. 1:20)

This verse shows us that the seven churches are a light to their regions. They enjoy the privilege of having Christ walk among them.

Jesus said in Matthew 5:14-16:

"You are the light of the world. A city that is set on a hill cannot be hidden. Nor do they light a lamp and put it under a basket, but on a lampstand, and it gives light to all who are in the house. Let your light so shine before men, that they may see your good works and glorify your Father in heaven."

A lampstand is a gift from God that grants a congregation intimacy with Christ and a magnetic power to reach a region.

I have witnessed up-close churches that were given just such a lampstand. I have watched them grow from very few in number to multiple thousands. It was amazing to watch as God would take a small group and then make them a magnetic force and a holy beam to an entire region. Masses would be drawn into their light.

.   I have also seen the horrible tragedy of a lampstand being removed. I have visited famous sanctuaries that once teemed with revival and are now empty and haunted by aching memories. God had repeatedly warned these churches to return to their first love, but they refused.

History shows us that not only churches but an entire nation can receive a lampstand. From the moment he was converted, Paul knew that he had to go to Rome. He knew, prophetically, that one day it would be the seat of the gospel for the entire world.

As the centuries went by, that lampstand was moved to England. The British church sent missionaries to all the known world. With the lampstand, England received many other blessings. She enjoyed supernatural protection. She enjoyed global prestige. She enjoyed powerful and wondrous prosperity. As time passed, it became agonizingly clear that England had lost her lampstand. England's decline as both a global superpower and an economic force coincided directly with her recession from honoring and advancing the gospel.

Next the lampstand moved to America. The United States exported the gospel as no nation before her had ever done. America was crowned with unsurpassed global prestige and wealth beyond imagination.

As I was praying recently, I heard the *violent voice of God.* It was unmistakable. It said, **"Tell America to return to her first love or I must remove the lampstand."** The crimes against God in our nation are now innumerable, starting with the obvious holocaust on the unborn, the militant efforts to erase the ethics of Christianity, and finally the persecution of the church.

What I say next, I say with great caution. I am certain that all of the Christians who voted for Bill Clinton did so because they felt he would do the best job, not because they endorse immorality in any way. Having said that, I must tell you that we would be blind not to see that millions of Americans and the media see Mr. Clinton's reelection as an endorsement of lower morals and a rejection of the family values movement. We cannot deny that millions used their votes for him to make a statement: *Expand abortion, curtail the Christian Coalition, remove the character issue, and relax attitudes toward sexual promiscuity.* ***The bottom line is that the electorate rejected the lampstand!***

In the next four years we can anticipate greater moral darkness because anti-Christian forces have been emboldened. They are seizing this moment to expand and intensify their agenda.

Expect federal intrusion into Christian churches as never before. Anticipate public schools to be much more free in their verbal attacks on the Christian faith and the Bible. Hollywood, too, will open the sludge valve sensing that America is ready for more filth.

As all of this is happening, there is a new phenomenon going on in the Orient. Korea, and the Christians who live there, are fast assuming a world leadership role in the faith. Massive numbers of believers pray in Korea in a way that American Christians cannot even imagine. Singapore is now home to a *holy wealth* that is filling the coffers of world evangelism neglected by the American church.

China, though politically oppressive, is home to a great revival that may end up being the greatest in the history of the world. The churches of Asia are flooding America with missionaries, just as we once sent missionaries to other nations.

There are a barrage of questions that burn in my heart:

- ***is the lampstand that moved to America from England about to move west again to the Orient?***
- ***is the Year 2000, which is not only the turn of the century but also a millennium, the natural point at which God will transfer the lampstand?***
- ***Will America, once proud and free, now take on a "second- rate nation" status?***
- ***Have we irreparably sinned away our future?***
- ***Can America's Christians ever get on fire and truly cry out to God that He would show mercy and rescind His decision to take our lampstand away?***
- ***Do we see how our Christian giving and generosity has become a cold, cynical, budget-ary act?***
- ***Can we admit that our self-centered teachings have pulled us away from world evangelism?***
- ***Will corrupted leaders ever face their hype and manipulation of crowds and violently repent before God before it is too late?***

My friend, I believe that this is our last chance, but I also believe that it is not too late. There are signs of hope! Tens of thousands of American Christians are making a pilgrimage to Pensacola, Florida to experience a fiery outpouring of the Holy Spirit that many believe is about to change our nation. Here is the amazing account of how God foretold this revival in Pensacola and how it would sweep America:

David Yonggi Cho of Seoul, Korea writes, "While I was ministering in Seattle, Washington, in 1991, I became deeply concerned about the spiritual decline in America. I began to pray even more earnestly for revival in these United States. As I prayed, I felt the Lord prompt me to get a map of America and point my finger on the map. I found myself pointing to the city of Pensacola in the Florida panhandle. Then I sensed the Lord say, 'I am going to send revival to the seaside city of Pensacola, and it will spread like a fire until all of America has been consumed by it.'"

Thousands of leaders have repented. Tens of thousands have found Christ. This great awakening is only one of many that are just now starting to be reported across America. This is the final great outpouring that God is sending to try to keep the lampstand in America. I believe that we can cause the heavens to bless America once more, but we must wholeheartedly respond to the message of the Holy Spirit to the American church:

God is commanding you to repent as an individual. Forget about the sins of others, the needs of others, or the mistakes of others. See only your private need for *a fresh fire* from God. You and you alone must fall before God, weep and confess, and ask for *fresh fire.* I believe you can repent privately, but I also believe that, if we delay repentance, the Lord will force us to repent before others,

146

so that we can receive this fire. Therefore, repent early, even as you are reading this. Fall on your face before the Lord and allow Him to touch you.

Align yourself with the forces of God for righteousness in America. We must speak out as one with those who are the obedient servants of God. We must speak to America, not in general terms, but in sharp, clear, loving, surgically accurate terms about the demands of God.

We must do away with spotty prayer and cry out to God with an undivided heart and an unbridled spirit. Nothing less than focused, fiery intercession matters at this moment in American history.

We must release our finances to God. We dare not use the abuses of the past as a license to strangle legitimate gospel ministry. If you have decided to horde your money now, will you then be forced to spend it in an evil, treacherous, and violent future America? The Holy Spirit does not want to move the lampstand from America, but after a deadline that only He knows, it will be moved. Jesus is seeking American disciples to prevail in prayer. God is looking for you! Let us discard the lukewarm life that has left us miserable anyway and collapse before our awesome and loving God. Let us rush in, fill the void, and be set on fire while there is still time. With all my heart, I am convinced that we can win this great war and prevail upon God to keep the lampstand in the United States of America!

Love, *Mario*

Printed By Permission from Mario Murillo Ministries

147

——— 2 ———

NINEVEH'S
REPENTANCE
AND
DELIVERANCE

Joseph Sewall

Joseph Sewall (1688-1769). A Harvard graduate of 1707,
Sewall spent a long and generally serene ministry at
Old South Church in Boston, where he preached beyond
his eightieth year.
Reprinted here is a fast-day sermon preached before the
Massachusetts governor, the council, and the house of
representatives on December 3, 1740.

BOSTON

1740

And GOD was pleas'd to fulfill his promise to his people, I Sam. 7. and in other instances upon record in scripture. In a word, the Lord Jesus our great high priest, has offered a sacrifice of infinite value to make atonement for the congregation of his people, whether Jews or gentiles; and he lives in heaven to interceed for them. And therefore, when GOD's people took to him and mourn and turn to the Lord, he will turn from his fierce anger, and command salvation.

APPLICATION

USE 1. Learn that *true religion lays the surest foundation of a people's prosperity. Righteousness exaltetb a Nation,* Prov. 14. 34- When we turn to GOD by Jesus Christ, and do works meet for repentance; we take the best way to obtain salvation from the help of his countenance, who is the Father of Lights, from whom cometh down every good & every perfect gift. It's sin that separateth between GOD and his people: When this accursed thing is therefore put away from among them, that GOD to whom belong the issues from death, will draw nigh to them with his saving health, and appear for their deliverance.

And if *GOD be for us, who can be against us? There is no Wisdom nor Understanding, nor Counsel against the Lord. The Horse is prepared against the Day of Battle: But Safety is of the Lord.* PROV 21. 30, 31. Certainly then, the one thing needful is to secure the presence and favour of GOD; and this we do when we return to him in hearty repentance, and then walk before him in new obedience. Blessed is that people whose GOD is the LORD: No weapon form'd against them shall prosper, and that good word shall be fulfilled unto them, *God is our Refuge and Strength, a very present Help in Trouble, Psal - 46. I and V. 5. God is in the midst of her, she shall not be moved. God shall help her, and that right early,* O that GOD would impress on our minds the firm belief of these things! O that he would affect our hearts suitably with them! That we might strive together in our prayers this day, crying to GOD with the prophet, *O Lord, revive thy Work in the midst of the Years, in the midst of the Years make known; in Wrath remember Mercy. Hab. 3. 2.*

USE 2. *Abounding iniquity will be the destruction of a people, except they repent.* If they persist and go on in the ways of sin, refusing to return to GOD, iniquity will be their ruin. *Sin is the Reproach of any People,* Prov. 14. 34. It hath both a natural and moral tendency to lay them low, and expose them to shame. Sin in the body politick, is like some foul and deadly disease in the natural body which turns the beauty of it into corruption, and weakens all it's powers. *Why should ye be stricken any more? ye will revolt more and more: the whole Head is sick, and the whole Heart is faint. From the Sole of the Foot, even unto the Crown of the Head, there is no Soundness in it; but Wounds and Bruises, and putrefying Sores: they have not been closed, neither bound up, neither molified with Ointment,* Isa. I. 5, 6. And then, this deadly evil provokes the holy GOD to pour contempt upon a people, and lay their honour in the dust. Thus GOD threatned his people, *Thou shalt become an Astonishment, a Proverb, and a By-word, among all Nations whither the Lord shall lead thee.* Deut. 28. 37. And in the 44th and 45th [verse:] *He shall lend to thee, and thou shalt not lend to him; he shall he the Head, and thou shalt he the Tail. Moreover all these Curses shall come upon thee, and overtake thee till thou he destroyed: Because thou hearknedst not unto the Voice of the Lord thy God, to keep his Commandments and his Statutes which he commanded thee.*

And the threatning was fulfilled upon them. GOD said to his people, O Israel, Thou hast fallen by thine iniquity. And the weeping prophet laments their sins and ruin, *Jerusalem hath grievously sinned: all that honoured her, despise her, because they have seen her nakedness: yea, she sigheth, and turneth backward. Her filthiness is in her skirts, she remembreth not her last end, therefore she came down wonderfully: she had no Comforter.* Yea, after this remarkable deliverance granted to Nineveh, it's suppos'd about ninety years, when they returned to their former sins, the prophet Nahum foretells their ruin, Chap. I.

USE 3. Let us then be sensible of the *destroying evil of sin,* and the *necessity of true repentance.*

GOD speaks to us this day as to his people of old, *Thine own wickedness shall correct thee, and thy Backslidings shall reprove thee: know therefore and see, that it is an evil thing and bitter that thou hast forsaken the Lord thy God, and that my fear is not in thee, saith the Lord God of hosts,* Jer. 2. 19. And as 44. 4. *O do not this abominable thing that I hate.* Most certainly they are guilty of great folly, who make a mock at sin. This is to cast fire-brands, arrows and death; and say, Am I not sport? The wise man observes, that *One Sinner destroyeth much Good,* Eccl. 9. 18. Thus *Achan took of the accursed Thing; and the Anger of the Lord was kindled against the Children of Israel,* Josh. 7- I. Let us then fly from sin as the most pernicious evil, and see the necessity of our turning to the Lord by sincere repentance. O let that word of the Lord sink deep into our hearts this day! *Turn ye, turn ye, Why will ye die, O House of Israel?* Ezek- 33- II-

Which leads me to the last use;

4. Let us all be exhorted *to turn, every one from his evil way; and to engage heartily in the necessary work of reformation. This, this is our great duty and interest this day, as we would hope to be made instruments in GOD's hand of saving our selves and this peoples Let us then seriously consider that we have to do with that GOD who is able to save and to destroy. And settle that word in our hearts as a certain truth, When he giveth Quietness, who then can make Trouble? and when he hideth his Face, who then can behold him? whether it be done against a Nation, or against a Man Only.* Job 34. 29. And accordingly, let us turn from all sin to the Lord, and in this way hope and wait for his salvation. O let us take heed, lest there be in any of *us an evil Heart of Unbelief in departing from the living God.* To day, let us hear his voice, and not harden our hearts. May each one of us say with job, *Now mine Eye seeth thee: Wherefore I abhor my self, and repent in Dust and Ashes.* And as it has pleased the Father to commit all judgment to the Son; let us look to him, and encourage our selves in him whom GOD hath exalted to be a *prince and a Saviour, to give repentance to Israel, and forgiveness of sins.* May our ascended JESUS, who has receiv'd of the Father the promise of the Holy Ghost, pour out this great blessing upon the whole land, and fulfill that word,

Then will I sprinkle clean Water upon you, and ye shall be clean: from all your filthiness and from all your Idols will I cleanse you. A new Heart also will I give you, and a new Spirit will I put within you, and I will take away the stony Heart out of your Flesh, and I will give you an Heart of Flesh. And I will put my Spirit within you, and cause you to walk in my Statutes, and ye shall keep my Judgments, and do them. And ye shall dwell in the Land that I gave to your Fathers, and ye shall be my People, and I will be your God. Ezek. 35. 25-28.

'My fathers! Suffer the word of exhortation: Let GOD see your works; that you turn from every evil way; that GOD May also repent of the evil, and not bring it upon us. For how dreadful must it be if the example of the nobles and men of Nineveh should rise up in judgment against any of you: They repented at the preaching "of one Prophet sent to them by GOD, you have Moses and the Prophets"; Yea in these last days GOD has spoken to us by his Son that prince of the prophets, who is GOD manifest in the flesh. You have the sacred writings of the New-Testament, in which GOD reveals his wrath against all ungodliness and unrighteousness of men; and also his grace and mercy to the penitent by a redeemer. And as the judge of all the earth hath advanced you to rule over his people; so he declareth to you in his word, That *they who rule over Men must be just, ruling in the Fear of GOD;* and requireth you to lead in the work of reformation by your example, and by the right use of that power with which he hath betrusted you.

And would you, our honoured rulers, to whom I again address myself, have the all-wise GOD present to shew you what his people ought to do in this very critical conjuncture, and to make you the joyful instruments of our deliverance; then abide with GOD by taking his word for your rule, by making his glory your highest end, and by seeking the public-weal in all things. Ask of GOD a public spirit, and by all means labour to subdue a vicious self-love remembring the warning given us, 2 Tim. 3. I, 2. *In the last Days perilous Times shall come. For Men shall be lovers of their own selves, covetous.* May you have the love of GOD and his people shed abroad in your hearts by his spirit; and be ready to sacrifice private views and personal interests to the publick good! Shake your hands from bribes of every kind, and when call'd to give your vote, consider seriously what is right in the sight of GOD, with whom is *no respect of persons, or taking of gifts;* and act accordingly. And if at any time you should be tempted to this great evil, as the best of men may; set that word of GOD in opposition to the temptation.

He that walketh righteously, and speaketh uprightly, he that despiseth the Gain of Oppression, that shaketh his Hands from holding of Bribes, that stoppeth his Ears from hearing of Blood, and shutteth his Eyes from seeing Evil: He shall dwell on high, his Place of Defence shall be the Munition of Rocks; Bread shall be given him, his Waters shall be sure. Isa. 33. 15, 16.

In this way you shall obtain the gracious presence of GOD with you. *The Lord is with you, while ye be with him,* 2. Chron. 15. 2. And if GOD be with you and for you, who can be against you? What can harm you? What can be too hard for you, if the Almighty is pleas'd to own you as his servants, and command deliverance for his people by you? Surely the mountains shall become a plain, crooked things straight, and the night shine as the day. Let me say to you therefore as 2 Chron. 15. 7. *Be ye strong, and let not your Hands be weak: for your Work shall be rewarded.* GOD will be your shield, and exceeding great reward. You shall see the good of GOD's chosen, rejoice with the gladness of his nation, and glory with his inheritance. And when the Son of Man shall come in his glory, and all the holy angels with him, then shall he say unto you, *Inasmuch as ye have done it unto these my Brethren, ye have done it unto me: Come ye Blessed of my Father, inherit the Kingdom.*

FINIS

The United States Constitution

Our God-Inspired Constitution

The Constitution of the United States is a document that was bathed in prayer by our founding fathers. For many days the framers of the constitution argued and debated about its organization and its wording. This led the entire New York delegation to leave the meetings altogether. Such disunity caused a pall of gloom to settle over the meetings.

Eighty-one-year-old Benjamin Franklin, so ill that he had to be carried into the meeting hall, stood to address the discouraged delegates. He reminded them of earlier meetings of the Provincial Congress which had always opened with prayer. In the first meeting of the Provincial Congress (in 1774), for example, the founding fathers met for more than three hours in earnest prayer for the nation and their deliberations before they began their planning. George Washington, John Adams, Patrick Henry and many other well-known leaders knelt before the Lord, seeking His blessings on America.

After reminding them of the power of prayer that they had experienced during the meetings of the Provincial Congress, Ben Franklin went on to call the delegates to the Constitutional Convention to intercession: "In the beginning of the contest with Great Britain, when we were sensible of danger, we had daily prayer in this room for divine protection. Our prayers, sir, were heard and they were graciously answered....And have we now forgotten this powerful Friend? Or do we imagine that we no longer need His assistance?

"I've lived, sir, a long time, and the longer I live, the more convincing proofs I see of this truth: That God governs in the affairs of men. If a sparrow cannot fall to the ground without His notice, is it probable that an empire can rise without His aid? We've been assured in the sacred writings that unless the Lord build the house, they labor in vain who build it. I firmly believe this, and I also believe that without His concurring aid, we shall succeed in this political building no better than the builders of Babel."

"I therefore beg leave to move that henceforth prayers imploring the assistance of Heaven and its blessing on our deliberations be held in this assembly every morning before we proceed to business."

As a result of Franklin's affirmation of the power of prayer in the Constitutional Convention, several wonderful and amazing things happened. The entire assembly of delegates participated in three days of prayer and fasting. They joined together and visited every church they could find in Philadelphia in order to seek God's face and hear His Word proclaimed. When they reconvened, many delegates later reported, every unfriendly feeling had been expelled! Unity was restored. The decision-making flowed without friction. It was a dramatic turning point for the development of our nation – and the U.S. Constitution was born!

Also, as a result of Franklin's call to prayer, chaplains were established in the House of Representatives and the Senate to ensure that God's blessings would be invoked before all their meetings.

Incidentally, at the earlier Congress Franklin referred to (the Provincial Congress of 1774), the delegates actually prayed the Word of God (Psalms 35, in fact) before they proceeded with their business. One verse of this Psalm of David states: "I will give thee thanks in the great congregation: I will praise thee among much people" (Ps. 35:18).

In the early days of our nation, the presidents and the congress frequently called the people to prayer, fasting and thanksgiving. Many national days of prayer were observed, and businesses would close in recognition of the nation's need for prayer. The U.S. Congress even went so far as to keep a record of answered prayers in the Congressional Record. May it be that way once again.

Let us follow the faith-filled, God-fearing example of our founding fathers as we, like them, learn to pray the Word of God for our nation.

Taken from *Prayers That Prevail for America*, Published by Victory House, Inc., Tulsa, OK. Used with permission of the publisher.

The Constitution of the United States

PREAMBLE

We, the people of the United States, in order to form a more perfect Union, establish justice, insure domestic tranquility, provide for the common defense, promote the general welfare, and secure the blessings of liberty to ourselves and our posterity, do ordain and establish this Constitution for the United States of America.

ARTICLE I

Section 1.   *Legislative powers; in whom vested.*

All legislative powers herein granted shall be vested in a Congress of the United States, which shall consist of a Senate and House of Representatives.

Section 2.   *House of Representatives, how and by whom chosen Qualifications of a Representative. Representatives and direct taxes, how apportioned. Enumeration. Vacancies to be filled. Power of choosing officers, and of impeachment.*

1.   *The House of Representatives shall be composed of members chosen every second year by the people of the several States, and the elector in each State shall have the qualifications requisite for electors of the most numerous branch of the State Legislature.*

2.   *No person shall be a Representative who shall not have attained to the age of twenty-five years, and been seven years a citizen of the United States, and who shall not, when elected, be an inhabitant of that State in which he shall be chosen.*

3.   *Representatives [and direct taxes] Altered by 16th Amendment shall be apportioned among the several States which may be included within this Union, according to their respective numbers, [which shall be determined by adding the whole number of free persons, including those bound to service for a term of years, and excluding Indians not taxed, three-fifths of all other persons.] Altered by 14th Amendment The actual enumeration shall be made within three years after the first meeting of the Congress of the United States, and within every subsequent term of ten years, in such manner as they shall by law direct. The number of Representatives shall not exceed one for every thirty thousand, but each State shall have at least one Representative; and until such enumeration shall be made, the State of New Hampshire shall be entitled to choose three, Massachusetts eight, Rhode Island and Providence Plantations one, Connecticut five, New York six, New Jersey four, Pennsylvania eight, Delaware one, Maryland six, Virginia ten, North Carolina five, South Carolina five, and Georgia three.*

4.   *When vacancies happen in the representation from any State, the Executive Authority thereof shall issue writs of election to fill such vacancies.*

5.   *The House of Representatives shall choose their Speaker and other officers; and shall have the sole power of impeachment.*

Section 3.   *Senators, how and by whom chosen. How classified. State Executive, when to make temporary appointments, in case, etc. Qualifications of a Senator. President of the Senate, his right to vote. President pro tem., and other officers of the Senate, how chosen. Power to try impeachments. When President is tried, Chief Justice to preside. Sentence.*

1.   *The Senate of the United States shall be composed of two Senators from each State, [chosen by the Legislature thereof,] Altered by 17th Amendment for six years; and each Senator shall have one vote.*

2.   *Immediately after they shall be assembled in consequence of the first election, they shall be divided as equally as may be into three classes. The seats of the Senators of the first class shall be vacated at the expiration of the second year, of the second class at the expiration of the fourth year, and of the third class at the expiration of the sixth year, so that one-third may be chosen every second year; [and if vacancies happen by resignation, or otherwise, during the recess of the Legislature of any State, the Executive thereof may make temporary appointments until the next meeting of the Legislature, which shall then fill such vacancies.]Altered by 17th Amendment*

3.   *No person shall be a Senator who shall not have attained to the age of thirty years, and been nine years a citizen of the United States, and who shall not, when elected, be an inhabitant of that State for which he shall be chosen.*

4.   *The Vice-President of the United States shall be President of the Senate, but shall have no vote, unless they be equally divided.*

5.   *The Senate shall choose their other officers, and also a President*pro tempore, *in the absence of the Vice President, or when he shall exercise the office of the President of the United States.*

6.   *The Senate shall have the sole power to try all impeachments. When sitting for that purpose, they shall be on oath or affirmation. When the President of the United States is tried, the Chief Justice shall preside: and no person shall be convicted without the concurrence of two-thirds of the members present.*

7.   *Judgment in cases of impeachment shall not extend further than to removal from office, and disqualification to hold and enjoy any office of honor, trust, or profit under the United States: but the party convicted shall nevertheless be liable and subject to indictment, trial, judgment and punishment, according to law.*

Section 4.   *Times, etc., of holding elections, how prescribed. One session in each year.*

1.   *The times, places and manner of holding elections for Senators and Representatives, shall be prescribed in each State by the Legislature thereof; but the Congress may at any time by law make or alter such regulations, except as to the places of choosing Senators.*

2. The Congress shall assemble at least once in every year, and such meeting shall be [on the first Monday in December,] Altered by 20th Amendment unless they by law appoint a different day.

Section 5. *Membership, Quorum, Adjournment, Rules, Power to punish or expel. Journal. Time of adjournment, how limited, etc.*

1. Each House shall be the judge of the elections, returns and qualifications of its own members, and a majority of each shall constitute a quorum to do business; but a smaller number may adjourn from day to day, and may be authorized to compel the attendance of absent members, in such manner, and under such penalties as each House may provide.

2. Each House may determine the rules of its proceedings, punish its members for disorderly behavior, and, with the concurrence of two-thirds, expel a member.

3. Each House shall keep a journal of its proceedings, and from time to time publish the same, excepting such parts as may in their judgment require secrecy; and the yeas and nays of the members of either House on any question shall, at the desire of one-fifth of those present, be entered on the journal.

4. Neither House, during the session of Congress, shall, without the consent of the other, adjourn for more than three days, nor to any other place than that in which the two Houses shall be sitting.

Section 6. *Compensation, Privileges, Disqualification in certain cases.*

1. The Senators and Representatives shall receive a compensation for their services, to be ascertained by law, and paid out of the Treasury of the United States. They shall in all cases, except treason, felony and breach of the peace, be privileged from arrest during their attendance at the session of their respective Houses, and in going to and returning from the same; and for any speech or debate in either House, they shall not be questioned in any other place.

2. No Senator or Representative shall, during the time for which he was elected, be appointed to any civil office under the authority of the United States, which shall have increased during such time; and no person holding any office under the United States, shall be a member of either House during his continuance in office.

Section 7. *House to originate all revenue bills. Veto. Bill may be passed by two-thirds of each House, notwithstanding, etc. Bill, not returned in ten days to become a law. Provisions as to orders, concurrent resolutions, etc.*

1. All bills for raising revenue shall originate in the House of Representatives; but the Senate may propose or concur with amendments as on other bills.

2. Every bill which shall have passed the House of Representatives and the Senate, shall, before it become a law, be presented to the president of the United States; if he approve, he shall sign it, but if not, he shall return it, with his objections, to that house in which it shall have originated, who shall enter the objections at large on their journal, and pro-

ceed to reconsider it. If after such reconsideration, two thirds of that house shall agree to pass the bill, it shall be sent, together with the objections, to the other house, by which it shall likewise be reconsidered, and if approved by two-thirds of that house, it shall become a law. But in all such cases the votes of both houses shall be determined by yeas and nays, and the names of the persons voting for and against the bill shall be entered on the journal of each house respectively. If any bill shall not be returned by the president within ten days (Sundays excepted) after it shall have been presented to him, the same shall be a law, in like manner as if he had signed it, unless the Congress by their adjournment prevent its return, in which case it shall not be a law.

3.   Every order, resolution, or vote to which the concurrence of the Senate and House of Representatives may be necessary (except on a question of adjournment) shall be presented to the president of the United States; and before the same shall take effect, shall be approved by him, or, being disapproved by him, shall be re-passed by two-thirds of the Senate and House of Representatives, according to the rules and limitations prescribed in the case of a bill.

Section 8.   *Powers of Congress*

The Congress shall have the power

1.   To lay and collect taxes, duties, imposts and excises, to pay the debts and provide for the common defence and general welfare of the United States; but all duties, imposts and excises shall be uniform throughout the United States:

2.   To borrow money on the credit of the United States:

3.   To regulate commerce with foreign nations, and among the several states, and with the Indian tribes:

4.   To establish an uniform rule of naturalization, and uniform laws on the subject of bankruptcies throughout the United States:

5.   To coin money, regulate the value thereof, and of foreign coin, and fix the standard of weights and measures:

6.   To provide for the punishment of counterfeiting the securities and current coin of the United States:

7.   To establish post-offices and post-roads:

8.   To promote the progress of science and useful arts, by securing for limited times to authors and inventors the exclusive right to their respective writings and discoveries:

9.   To constitute tribunals inferior to the supreme court:

10.   To define and punish piracies and felonies committed on the high seas, and offenses against the law of nations:

11.   To declare war, grant letters of marque and reprisal, and make rules concerning captures on land and water:

12. *To raise and support armies, but no appropriation of money to that use shall be for a longer term than two years:*

13. *To provide and maintain a navy:*

14. *To make rules for the government and regulation of the land and naval forces:*

15. *To provide for calling forth the militia to execute the laws of the union, suppress insurrections and repel invasions:*

16. *To provide for organizing, arming and disciplining the militia, and for governing such part of them as may be employed in the service of the United States, reserving to the states respectively, the appointment of the officers, and the authority of training the militia according to the discipline prescribed by Congress:*

17. *To exercise exclusive legislation in all cases whatsoever, over such district (not exceeding ten miles square) as may, by cession of particular states, and the acceptance of Congress, become the seat of the government of the United States, and to exercise like authority over all places purchased by the consent of the legislature of the state in which the same shall be, for the erection of forts, magazines, arsenals, dock-yards, and other needful buildings: And,*

18. *To make all laws which shall be necessary and proper for carrying into execution the foregoing powers, and all other powers vested by this constitution in the government of the United States, or in any department or officer thereof.*

Section 9.   *Provision as to migration or importation of certain persons.* **Habeas Corpus,** *Bills of attainder, etc.* **Taxes, how apportioned. No export duty. No commercial preference. Money, how drawn from Treasury, etc. No titular nobility. Officers not top receive presents, etc.**

1. *The migration or importation of such persons as any of the states now existing shall think proper to admit, shall not be prohibited by the Congress prior to the year 1808, but a tax or duty may be imposed on such importations, not exceeding 10 dollars for each person.*

2. *The privilege of the writ of* habeas corpus *shall not be suspended, unless when in cases of rebellion or invasion the public safety may require it.*

3. *No bill of attainder or* ex post facto *law shall be passed.*

4. *[No capitation, or other direct tax shall be laid unless in proportion to the census or enumeration herein before directed to be taken.] Altered by 16th Amendment*

5. *No tax or duty shall be laid on articles exported from any state.*

6. *No preference shall be given by any regulation of commerce or revenue to the ports of one state over those of another: nor shall vessels bound to, or from one state, be obliged to enter, clear, or pay duties in another.*

7. *No money shall be drawn from the treasury but in consequence of appropriations made by law; and a regular statement and account of the receipts and expenditures of all public money shall be published from time to time.*

8. *No title of nobility shall be granted by the United States: And no person holding any office or profit or trust under them, shall, without the consent of the Congress, accept of any present, emolument, office, or title, of any kind whatever, from any king, prince, or foreign state.*

Section 10. *States prohibited from the exercise of certain powers.*

1. *No state shall enter into any treaty, alliance, or confederation; grant letters of marque and reprisal; coin money; emit bills of credit; make any thing but gold and silver coin a tender in payment of debts; pass any bill of attainder,* ex post facto *law, or law impairing the obligation of contracts, or grant any title of nobility.*

2. *No state shall, without the consent of the Congress, lay any imposts or duties on imports or exports, except what may be absolutely necessary for executing its inspection laws; and the net produce of all duties and imposts, laid by any state on imports or exports, shall be for the use of the treasury of the United States; and all such laws shall be subject to the revision and control of the Congress.*

3. *No state shall, without the consent of Congress, lay any duty of tonnage, keep troops, or ships of war in time of peace, enter into any agreement or compact with another state, or with a foreign power, or engage in a war, unless actually invaded, or in such imminent danger as will not admit of delay.*

ARTICLE II

Section 1. *President: his term of office. Electors of President; number and how appointed. Electors to vote on same day. Qualification of President. On whom his duties devolve in case of his removal, death, etc. President's compensation. His oath of office.*

1. *The Executive power shall be vested in a President of the United States of America. He shall hold office during the term of four years, and together with the Vice President, chosen for the same term, be elected as follows*

2. *[Each State] Altered by 23rd Amendment shall appoint, in such manner as the Legislature may direct, a number of electors, equal to the whole number of Senators and Representatives to which the State may be entitled in the Congress: but no Senator or Representative, or person holding an office of trust or profit under the United States, shall be appointed an elector [The electors shall meet in their respective States, and vote by ballot for two persons, of whom one at least shall not be an inhabitant of the same State with themselves. And they shall make a list of all the persons voted for each; which list they shall sign and certify, and transmit sealed to the seat of Government of the United States, directed to the President of the Senate. The President of the Senate shall, in the presence of the Senate and House of Representatives, open all the certificates, and the votes shall*

164

then be counted. *The person having the greatest number of votes shall be the President, if such number be a majority of the whole number of electors appointed; and if there be more than one who have such majority, and have an equal number of votes, then the House of Representatives shall immediately choose by ballot one of them for President; and if no person have a majority, then from the five highest on the list the said House shall in like manner choose the President. But in choosing the President, the votes shall be taken by States, the representation from each State having one vote; a quorum for this purpose shall consist of a member or members from two-thirds of the States, and a majority of all the States shall be necessary to a choice. In every case, after the choice of the President, the person having the greatest number of votes of the electors shall be the Vice President. But if there should remain two or more who have equal votes, the Senate shall choose from them by ballot the Vice President.] Altered by 12th Amendment*

3. *The Congress may determine the time of choosing the electors, and the day on which they shall give their votes; which day shall be the same throughout the United States.*

4. *No person except a natural born citizen, or a citizen of the United States, at the time of the adoption of this Constitution, shall be eligible to the office of President; neither shall any person be eligible to that office who shall not have attained to the age of thirty-five years, and been fourteen years a resident within the United States.*

5. *[In case of the removal of the President from office, or of his death, resignation, or inability to discharge the powers and duties of the said office, the same shall devolve on the Vice President, and the Congress may by law provide for the case of removal, death, resignation, or inability, both of the President and Vice President, declaring what officer shall then act as President, and such officer shall act accordingly, until the disability be removed, or a President shall be elected.] Altered by 25th Amendment*

6. *The President shall, at stated times, receive for his services, a compensation, which shall neither be increased nor diminished during the period for which he shall have been elected, and he shall not receive within that period any other emolument from the United States, or any of them.*

7. *Before he enter on the execution of his office, he shall take the following oath or affirmation:*

"I do solemnly swear (or affirm) that I will faithfully execute the office of the President of the United States, and will to the best of my ability, preserve, protect and defend the Constitution of the United States."

Section 2. ***President to be Commander-in-Chief. He may require opinions of cabinet officers, etc., may pardon. Treaty-making power. Nomination of certain officers. When President may fill vacancies.***

1. *The President shall be Commander-in-Chief of the Army and Navy of the United States, and of the militia of the several States, when called into the actual service of the United States; he may require the opinion, in writing, of the principal officer in each of the executive departments, upon any subject relating to the duties of their respective offices, and he shall have power to grant reprieves and pardons for offenses against against the United States, except in cases of impeachment.*

2.   *He shall have power, by and with the advice and consent of the Senate, to make treaties, provided two-thirds of the Senators present concur; and he shall nominate, and by and with the advice and consent of the Senate, shall appoint ambassadors, other public ministers and consuls, judges of the Supreme Court, and all other officers of the United States, whose appointments are not herein otherwise provided for, and which shall be established by law: but the Congress may by law vest the appointment of such inferior officers, as they think proper, in the President alone, in the courts of law, or in the heads of departments.*

3.   *The President shall have the power to fill up all vacancies that may happen during the recess of the Senate, by granting commissions, which shall expire at the end of their next session.*

Section 3.   *President shall communicate to Congress. He may convene and adjourn Congress, in case of disagreement, etc. Shall receive ambassadors, execute laws, and commission officers.*

He shall from time to time give to the Congress information of the state of the Union, and recommend to their consideration such measures as he shall judge necessary and expedient; he may, on extraordinary occasions, convene both Houses, or either of them, and in case of disagreement between them, with respect to the time of adjournment, he may adjourn them to such time as he shall think proper; he may receive ambassadors, and other public ministers; he shall take care that the laws be faithfully executed, and shall commission all the officers of the United States.

Section 4.   *All civil offices forfeited for certain crimes.*

The President, Vice President, and all civil officers of the United States, shall be removed from office on impeachment for, and conviction of, treason, bribery, or other high crimes and misdemeanors.

ARTICLE III

Section 1.   *Judicial powers. Tenure. Compensation.*

The judicial power of the United States, shall be vested in one supreme court, and in such inferior courts as the Congress may, from time to time, ordain and establish. The judges, both of the supreme and inferior courts, shall hold their offices during good behavior, and shall, at stated times, receive for their services a compensation, which shall not be diminished during their continuance in office.

Section 2.   *Judicial power; to what cases it extends. Original jurisdiction of Supreme Court Appellate. Trial by Jury, etc. Trial, where*

1.   *The judicial power shall extend to all cases, in law and equity, arising under this constitution, the laws of the United States, and treaties made, or which shall be made under their authority; to all cases affecting ambassadors, other public ministers and consuls; to all cases of admiralty and maritime jurisdiction; to controversies to which the United States shall be a party; [to controversies between two or more states, between a state and citizens of another state, between citizens of different states, between citizens of the same*

state, claiming lands under grants of different states, and between a state, or the citizens thereof, and foreign states, citizens or subjects.] Altered by 11th Amendment

2.   *In all cases affecting ambassadors, other public ministers and consuls, and those in which a state shall be a party, the supreme court shall have original jurisdiction. In all the other cases before-mentioned, the supreme court shall have appellate jurisdiction, both as to law and fact, with such exceptions, and under such regulations as the Congress shall make.*

3.   *The trial of all crimes, except in cases of impeachment, shall be by jury; and such trial shall be held in the state where the said crimes shall have been committed; but when not committed within any state, the trial shall be at such place or places as the Congress may by law have directed.*

Section 3.   *Treason defined. Proof of. Punishment*

1.   *Treason against the United States shall consist only in levying war against them, or in adhering to their enemies, giving them aid and comfort. No person shall be convicted of treason unless on the testimony of two witnesses to the same overt act, or on confession in open court.*

2.   *The Congress shall have power to declare the punishment of treason, but no attainder of treason shall work corruption of blood, or forfeiture, except during the life of the person attained.*

ARTICLE IV

Section 1.   *Each State to give credit to the public acts, etc. of every other State.*

Full faith and credit shall be given in each state to the public acts, records and judicial proceedings of every other state. And the Congress may by general laws prescribe the manner in which such acts, records and proceedings shall be proved, and the effect thereof.

Section 2.   *Privileges of citizens of each State. Fugitives from Justice to be delivered up. Persons held to service having escaped, to be delivered up.*

1.   *The citizens of each state shall be entitled to all privileges and immunities of citizens in the several states. See the 14th Amendment*

2.   *A person charged in any state with treason, felony, or other crime, who shall flee justice, and be found in another state, shall, on demand of the executive authority of the state from which he fled, be delivered up, to be removed to the state having jurisdiction of the crime.*

3.   *[No person held to service or labour in one state, under the laws thereof, escaping into another, shall, in consequence of any law or regulation therein, be discharged from such*

service or labour, but shall be delivered up on claim of the party to whom such service or labour may be due.] Altered by 13th Amendment

Section 3.   *Admission of new States. Power of Congress over territory and other property.*

1.   *New states may be admitted by the Congress into this union; but no new state shall be formed or erected within the jurisdiction of any other state, nor any state be formed by the junction of two or more states, without the consent of the legislatures of the states concerned, as well as of the Congress.*

2.   *The Congress shall have power to dispose of and make all needful rules and regulations respecting the territory or other property belonging to the United States; and nothing in this constitution shall be so construed as to prejudice any claims of the United States, or of any particular state.*

Section 4.   *Republican form of government guaranteed. Each State to be protected.*

The United States shall guarantee to every state in this union, a republican form of government, and shall protect each of them against invasion; and on application of the legislature, or of the executive (when the legislature cannot be convened), against domestic violence.

ARTICLE V

Amendments

The Congress, whenever two-thirds of both houses shall deem it necessary, shall propose amendments to this constitution, or on the application of the legislatures of two-thirds of the several states, shall call a convention for proposing amendments, which, in either case, shall be valid to all intents and purposes, as part of this constitution, when ratified by the legislatures of three-fourths of the several states, or by conventions in three-fourths thereof, as the one or the other mode of ratification may be proposed by the Congress: Provided, that no amendment which may be made prior to the year 1808, shall in any manner affect the first and fourth clauses in the ninth section of the first article; and that no state, without its consent, shall be deprived of its equal suffrage in the Senate.

ARTICLE VI

1. All debts contracted and engagements entered into, before the adoption of this constitution, shall be as valid against the United States under this constitution, as under the confederation. 2. This constitution, and the laws of the United States which shall be made in pursuance thereof; and all treaties made, or which shall be made, under the authority of the United States shall be the supreme law of the land; and the judges in every state shall be bound thereby, any thing in the constitution or laws of any state to the contrary notwithstanding. 3. The senators and representatives before-mentioned, and the members of the several state legislatures, and all executive and judicial officers, both of the United States and of the several states, shall be bound by oath or affirmation, to support this constitution; but no religious test shall ever be required as a qualification to any office or public trust under the United States.

ARTICLE VII

The ratification of the conventions of nine states, shall be sufficient for the establishment of this constitution between the states so ratifying the same.

AMENDMENTS

The Ten Original Amendments: The Bill of Rights. Proposed by Congress September 25, 1789. Ratified December 15, 1791.

Bill of Rights

AMENDMENT I

Congress shall make no law respecting an establishment of religion, or prohibiting the free exercise thereof; or abridging the freedom of speech, or of the press; or the right of the people peaceably to assemble, and to petition the Government for a redress of grievances.

AMENDMENT II

A well-regulated militia, being necessary to the security of a free State, the right of the people to keep and bear arms, shall not be infringed.

AMENDMENT III

No soldier shall, in time of peace be quartered in any house, without the consent of the owner, nor in time of war, but in a manner to be prescribed by law.

AMENDMENT IV

The right of the people to be secure in their persons, houses, papers, and effects, against unreasonable searches and seizures, shall not be violated, and no warrants shall issue, but upon probable cause, supported by oath or affirmation, and particularly describing the place to be searched, and the persons or things to be seized.

AMENDMENT V

No person shall be held to answer for a capital, or otherwise infamous crime, unless on a presentment or indictment of a Grand Jury, except in cases arising in the land or naval forces, or in the militia, when in actual service in time of war or public danger; nor shall any person be subject for the same offense to be twice put in jeopardy of life or limb; nor shall be compelled in any criminal case to be a witness against himself, nor be deprived of life, liberty, or property, without due process of law; nor shall private property be taken for public use without just compensation.

AMENDMENT VI

In all criminal prosecutions, the accused shall enjoy the right to a speedy and public trial, by an impartial jury of the State and district wherein the crime shall have been committed, which district shall have been previously ascertained by law, and to be informed of the nature and cause of the accusation; to be confronted with the witnesses against him; to have compulsory process for obtaining witnesses in his favor, and to have the assistance of counsel for his defense.

AMENDMENT VII

In suits at common law, where the value in controversy shall exceed twenty dollars, the right of trial by jury shall be preserved, and no fact tried by a jury shall be otherwise reexamined in any court of the United States, than according to the rules of the common law.

AMENDMENT VIII

Excessive bail shall not be required, nor excessive fines imposed, nor cruel and unusual punishments inflicted.

AMENDMENT IX

The enumeration in the Constitution, of certain rights, shall not be construed to deny or disparage others retained by the people.

AMENDMENT X

The powers not delegated to the United States by the Constitution, nor prohibited by it to the States, are reserved to the States respectively, or to the people.

End of the Bill of Rights

AMENDMENT XI

(Proposed by Congress March 4, 1794. Ratified February 7, 1795.)

The judicial power of the United States shall not be construed to extend to any suit in law or equity, commenced or prosecuted against one of the United States by citizens of another State, or by citizens or subjects of any foreign state.

AMENDMENT XII

(Proposed by Congress December 9, 1803. Ratified July 27, 1804.)

The Electors shall meet in their respective States and vote by ballot for President and Vice-President, one of whom, at least, shall not be an inhabitant of the same State with themselves; they shall name in their ballots the person voted for as President, and in distinct ballots the person voted for as Vice-President, and of the number of votes for each, which lists they shall sign and certify, and transmit sealed to the seat of the Government of the United States, directed to the President of the Senate; the President of the Senate shall, in the presence of the Senate and House of Representatives, open all the certificates and the votes shall then be counted; The person having the greatest number of votes for President, shall be the President, if such number be a majority of the whole number of Electors appointed; and if no person have such majority, then from the persons having the highest numbers not exceeding three on the list of those voted for as President, the House of Representatives shall choose immediately, by ballot, the President. But in choosing the President, the votes shall be taken by States, the representation from each State having one vote; a quorum for this purpose shall consist of a member or members from two-thirds of the States, and a majority of all the States shall be necessary to a choice. And if the House of Representatives shall not choose a President whenever the right of choice shall devolve upon them, [before the fourth day of March next following,] Altered by 20th Amendment then the Vice-President shall act as President, as in case of the death or other constitutional disability of the President. The person having the greatest number of votes as Vice-President, shall be the Vice-President, if such numbers be a majority of the whole number of electors appointed, and if no person have a majority, then from the two highest numbers on the list, the Senate shall choose the Vice-President; a quorum for the purpose shall consist of two-thirds of the whole number of Senators, and a majority of the whole number shall be necessary to a choice. But no person constitutionally ineligible to the office of President shall be eligible to that of Vice-President of the United States.

AMENDMENT XIII

(Proposed by Congress January 31, 1865. Ratified December 6, 1865.)

Section 1.   Neither slavery nor involuntary servitude, except as a punishment for crime whereof the party shall have been duly convicted, shall exist within the United States, or any place subject to their jurisdiction.

Section 2.   *Congress shall have power to enforce this article by appropriate legislation.*

AMENDMENT XIV

(Proposed by Congress June 13, 1866. Ratified July 9, 1868)

Section 1.   *All persons born or naturalized in the United States, and subject to the jurisdiction thereof, are citizens of the United States and of the State wherein they reside. No State shall make or enforce any law which shall abridge the privileges or immunities of citizens of the United States; nor shall any State deprive any person of life, liberty, or property, without due process of law; nor to deny to any person within its jurisdiction the equal protection of the laws.*

Section 2.   *Representatives shall be apportioned among the several States according to their respective numbers, counting the whole number of persons in each State, excluding Indians not taxed. But when the right to vote at any election for the choice of Electors for President and Vice-President of the United States, Representatives in Congress, the executive and judicial officers of a State, or the members of the Legislature thereof, is denied to any of the male inhabitants of such State, being twenty-one years of age, and citizens of the United States, or in any way abridged, except for participation in rebellion, or other crime, the basis of representation therein shall be reduced in the proportion which the number of such male citizens shall bear to the whole number of male citizens twenty-one years of age in such State.*

Section 3.   *No person shall be a Senator or Representative in Congress, or Elector of President and Vice-President, or hold any office, civil or military, under the United States, or under any State, who, having previously taken an oath, as a member of Congress, or as an officer of the United States, or as a member of any State Legislature, or as an executive or judicial officer of any State, to support the Constitution of the United States, shall have engaged in insurrection or rebellion against the same, or given aid or comfort to the enemies thereof. But Congress may by a vote of two-thirds of each House, remove such disability.*

Section 4.   *The validity of the public debt of the United States, authorized by law, including debts incurred for payment of pensions and bounties* for services in suppressing insurrection or rebellion, shall not be questioned. But neither the United States nor any State shall assume or pay any debt or obligation incurred in aid of insurrection or rebellion against the United States, or any claim for the loss or emancipation of any slave; but all such debts, obligations and claims shall be held illegal and void.

Section 5.   *The Congress shall have the power to enforce, by appropriate legislation, the provisions of this article.*

AMENDMENT XV

(Proposed by Congress February 26, 1869. Ratified February 3, 1870.)

Section 1.   *The right of citizens of the United States to vote shall not be denied or abridged by the United States or by any State on account of race, color, or previous condition of servitude.*
Section 2. The Congress shall have the power to enforce this article by appropriate legislation.

AMENDMENT XVI

(Proposed by Congress July 2, 1909. Ratified February 3, 1913.)

The Congress shall have power to lay and collect taxes on incomes, from whatever sources derived, without apportionment among the several States, and without regard to any census or enumeration.

AMENDMENT XVII

(Proposed by Congress May 13, 1912. Ratified April 8, 1913.)

The Senate of the United States shall be composed of two Senators from each State, elected by the people thereof, for six years; and each Senator shall have one vote. The electors in each State shall have the qualifications requisite for electors of the most numerous branch of the State Legislatures.

When vacancies happen in the representation of any State in the Senate, the executive authority of such State shall issue writs of election to fill such vacancies: Provided, That the Legislature of any State may empower the Executive thereof to make temporary appointments until the people fill the vacancies by election as the Legislature may direct.

This amendment shall not be so construed as to affect the election or term of any Senator chosen before it becomes valid as part of the Constitution.

AMENDMENT XVIII

(Proposed by Congress December 18, 1917. Ratified January 16, 1919. Altered by Amendment 21)

After one year from the ratification of this article the manufacture, sale, or transportation of intoxicating liquors within, the importation thereof into, or the exportation thereof from the United States and all territory subject to the jurisdiction thereof for beverage purposes is hereby prohibited.

The Congress and the several States shall have concurrent power to enforce this article by appropriate legislation.

This article shall be inoperative unless it shall have been ratified as an amendment to the Constitution by the Legislatures of the several States, as provided in the Constitution, within seven years from the date of the submission hereof to the States by the Congress.

AMENDMENT XIX

(Proposed by Congress June 4, 1919. Ratified August 18, 1920.)

The right of citizens of the United States to vote shall not be denied or abridged by the United States or by any State on account of sex. Congress shall have power to enforce this article by appropriate legislation.

AMENDMENT XX

Section 1.   The terms of the President and the Vice-President shall end at noon on the 20th day of January, and the terms of Senators and Representatives at noon on the 3rd day of January, of the years in which such terms would have ended if this article had not been ratified; and the terms of their successors shall then begin.

Section 2.   The Congress shall assemble at least once in every year, and such meeting shall begin at noon on the 3rd day of January, unless they shall by law appoint a different day.

Section 3.   If, at the time fixed for the beginning of the term of the President, the President elect shall have died, the Vice-President elect shall become President. If a President shall not have been chosen before the time fixed for the beginning of his term, or if the President elect shall have failed to qualify, then the Vice-President elect shall act as President until a President shall have qualified; and the Congress may by law provide for the case wherein neither a President elect nor a Vice-President shall have qualified, declaring who shall then act as President, or the manner in which one who is to act shall be selected, and such person shall act accordingly until a President or Vice-President shall have qualified.

Section 4.   The Congress may by law provide for the case of the death of any of the persons from whom the House of representatives may choose a President whenever the right of choice shall have devolved upon them, and for the case of the death of any of the persons from whom the Senate may choose a Vice-President whenever the right of choice shall have devolved upon them.

Section 5.   Sections 1 and 2 shall take effect on the 15th day of October following the ratification of this article (October 1933).

Section 6.   This article shall be inoperative unless it shall have been ratified as an amendment to the Constitution by the Legislatures of three-fourths of the several States within seven years from the date of its submission.

AMENDMENT XXI

(Proposed by Congress February 20, 1933. Ratified December 5, 1933.)

Section 1.   The Eighteenth article of amendment to the Constitution of the United States is hereby repealed.

Section 2.   The transportation or importation into any State, Territory, or Possession of the United States for delivery or use therein of intoxicating liquors, in violation of the laws thereof, is hereby prohibited.

Section 3.   This article shall be inoperative unless it shall have been ratified as an amendment to the Constitution by conventions in the several States, as provided in the Constitution, within seven years from the date of the submission hereof to the States by the Congress.

AMENDMENT XXII

(Proposed by Congress March 21, 1947. Ratified February 27, 1951.)

No person shall be elected to the office of the President more than twice, and no person who has held the office of President, or acted as President, for more that two years of a term to which *some other person was elected President shall be elected to the office of President more that once.*

But this Article shall not apply to any person holding the office of President when this Article was proposed by Congress, and shall not prevent any person who may be holding the office of President, or acting as President, during the term the term within which this Article becomes operative from holding the office of President or acting as President during the remainder of such term.

This article shall be inoperative unless it shall have been ratified as an amendment to the Constitution by the Legislatures of three-fourths of the several States within seven years from the date of its submission to the States by the Congress.

AMENDMENT XXIII

(Proposed by Congress June 16, 1960. Ratified March 29, 1961.)

Section 1.   *The District constituting the seat of Government of the United States shall appoint in such manner as Congress may direct:*
A number of electors of President and Vice President equal to the whole number of Senators and Representatives in Congress to which the District would be entitled if it were a State, but in no event more than the least populous State; they shall be in addition to those appointed by the States, but they shall be considered, for the purposes of the election of President and Vice President, to be electors appointed by a State; and they shall meet in the District and preform such duties as provided by the twelfth article of amendment.

Section 2.   *The Congress shall have power to enforce this article by appropriate legislation.*

AMENDMENT XXIV

(Proposed by Congress August 27, 1962. Ratified January 23, 1964.)

Section 1.   *The right of citizens of the United States to vote in any primary or other election for President or Vice President, for electors for President or Vice President, or for Senator or Representative in Congress, shall not be denied or abridged by the United States or any State by reason of failure to pay poll tax or any other tax.*

Section 2.   *Congress shall have power to enforce this article by appropriate legislation.*

AMENDMENT XXV

(Proposed by Congress July 6, 1965. Ratified February 10, 1967.)

Section 1.   *In case of the removal of the President from office or of his death or resignation, the Vice President shall become President.*

Section 2.   *Whenever there is a vacancy in the office of the Vice President, the President shall nominate a Vice President who shall take the office upon confirmation by a majority vote of both houses of Congress.*

Section 3.   *Whenever the President transmits to the President Pro tempore of the Senate and the Speaker of the House of Representatives his written declaration that he is unable to discharge the powers and duties of his office, and until he transmits to them a written declaration to the contrary, such powers and duties shall be discharged by the Vice President as Acting President.*

Section 4.   *Whenever the Vice President and a majority of either the principal officers of the executive departments or of such other body as Congress may by law provide, transmits to the President Pro tempore of the Senate and the Speaker of the House of Representatives their written declaration that the President is unable to discharge the powers and duties of his office, the Vice President shall immediately assume the powers and duties of the office as Acting President. Thereafter, when the President transmits to the President Pro tempore of the Senate and the Speaker of the House of Representatives his written declaration that no inability exists, he shall resume the powers and duties of his office unless the Vice President and a majority of either the principal officers of the executive departments or of such other body as Congress may by law provide, transmits within four days to the President Pro tempore of the Senate and the Speaker of the House of Representatives their written declaration that the President is unable to discharge the powers and duties of his office. Thereupon Congress shall decide the issue, assembling within forty-eight hours for that purpose if not in session. If the Congress, within twenty-one days after receipt of the latter written declaration, or, if Congress is not in session within twenty-one days after Congress is required to assemble, determines by two-thirds vote of both houses that the President is unable to discharge the powers and duties of his office, the Vice President shall continue to discharge the same as Acting President; otherwise, the President shall resume the powers and duties of his office.*

AMENDMENT XXVI

(Proposed by Congress March 23, 1971. Ratified June 30, 1971.)

Section 1.   *The right of citizens of the United States, who are 18 years of age or older, to vote shall not be denied or abridged by the United States or any state on account of age.*

Section 2.   *The Congress shall have power to enforce this article by appropriate legislation.*

AMENDMENT XXVII

(Proposed by Congress September 25, 1789. Ratified May 8, 1992)

No law, varying the compensation for the services of the Senators and Representatives, shall take effect, until an election of Representatives shall have intervened.

The Declaration of Independence

AMERICA'S DECLARATION OF INDEPENDENCE:

A Christian Legacy

Because of their belief in creation, the Declaration's drafters claimed that man's Creator gave him certain absolute rights. Not only do both the Old and New Testaments identify God as man's Creator **[Isaiah 40:28 and 1 Peter 4:19]**. They, also, identify God as the Giver of the three great rights listed in the Declaration: Life **[Genesis 2:7]**, Liberty **[II Corinthians 3:17]**, and the pursuit of Happiness **[Ecclesiastes 3:13]**. And the Bible confirms that what God has given shall not be taken away **[II Cronicles 19:7]**.

In the body of the Declaration, America's leaders presented their legal claims against King George III that they believed justified their fight for independence. By appealing to "the Supreme Judge of the world," they took their case for "freedom and independence" to God, Himself. In doing so, they followed the example of one of Israel's early leaders as recorded in Chapter 11 of the book of Judges.

Because they were, also, risking their personal lives and fortunes should the war be lost, the drafters affirmed their reliance on "Divine Providence" as their only assurance of protection. In doing so, they followed the example of Moses as he led the people out of Egypt to freedom.

Printed by permission from the Plymouth Rock Foundation
Fisk Mill, PO Box 425, Marlborough, New Hampshire 03455

The Declaration of Independence of the Thirteen Colonies

In CONGRESS, July 4, 1776

The unanimous Declaration of the thirteen united States of America,

When in the Course of human events, it becomes necessary for one people to dissolve the political bands which have connected them with another, and to assume among the powers of the earth, the separate and equal station to which the Laws of Nature and of Nature's God entitle them, a decent respect to the opinions of mankind requires that they should declare the causes which impel them to the separation.

We hold these truths to be self-evident, that all men are created equal, that they are endowed by their Creator with certain unalienable Rights, that among these are Life, Liberty, and the pursuit of Happiness. That to secure these rights, Governments are instituted among Men, deriving their just powers from the consent of the governed. That whenever any Form of Government becomes destructive of these ends, it is the Right of the People to alter or to abolish it, and to institute new Government, laying its foundation on such principles and organizing its powers in such form, as to them shall seem most likely to effect their Safety and Happiness.

Prudence, indeed, will dictate that Governments long established should not be changed for light and transient causes; and accordingly all experience hath shewn, that mankind are more disposed to suffer, while evils are sufferable, than to right themselves by abolishing the forms to which they are accustomed.

But when a long train of abuses and usurpations, pursuing invariably the same object evinces a design to reduce them under absolute Despotism, it is their right, it is their duty, to throw off such Government, and to provide new Guards for their future security.

Such has been the patient sufferance of these Colonies; and such is now the necessity which constrains them to alter their former Systems of Government. The history of the present King of Great Britain [George III] is a history of repeated injuries and usurpations, all having in direct object the establishment of an absolute Tyranny over these States. To prove this, let Facts be submitted to a candid world.

He has refused his Assent to Laws, the most wholesome and necessary for the public good.

He has forbidden his Governors to pass Laws of immediate and pressing importance, unless suspended in their operation till his Assent should be obtained, and when so suspended, he has utterly neglected to attend to them.

He has refused to pass other Laws for the accommodation of large districts of people, unless those people would relinquish the right of Representation in the Legislature, a right inestimable to them and formidable to tyrants only.

He has called together legislative bodies at places unusual, uncomfortable, and distant from the depository of their public Records, for the sole purpose of fatiguing them into compliance with his measures.

He has dissolved Representative Houses repeatedly, for opposing with manly firmness his invasions on the rights of the people.

He has refused for a long time, after such dissolutions, to cause others to be elected; whereby the Legislative powers, incapable of Annihilation, have returned to the People at large for their exercise; the State remaining in the meantime exposed to all the dangers of invasion from without, and convulsions within.

He has endeavoured to prevent the population of these States; for that purpose obstructing the Laws for Naturalization of Foreigners; refusing to pass others to encourage their migrations hither, and raising the conditions of new Appropriations of Lands.

He has obstructed the Administration of Justice, by refusing his Assent to Laws for establishing Judiciary powers.

He has made Judges dependent on his Will alone, for the tenure of their offices, and the amount and payment of their salaries.

He has erected a multitude of New Offices, and sent hither swarms of Officers to harass our people, and eat out their substance.

He has kept among us, in times of peace, Standing Armies, without the consent of our legislatures.

He has affected to render the Military independent of and superior to the Civil power.

He has combined with others to subject us to a jurisdiction foreign to our constitution and unacknowledged by our laws; giving his Assent to their Acts of pretended Legislation:

For protecting them by a mock Trial from punishment for any Murders which they should commit on the Inhabitants of these States:

For cutting off our Trade with all parts of the world:

For imposing Taxes on us without our Consent:

For depriving us in many cases of the benefits of Trial by Jury:

For transporting us beyond Seas to be tried for pretended offences:

For abolishing the free System of English Laws in a neighbouring Province, establishing therein an Arbitrary government, and enlarging its Boundaries so as to render it at once an example and fit instrument for introducing the same absolute rule into these Colonies:

For taking away our Charters, abolishing our most valuable Laws and altering fundamentally the Forms of our Governments:

For suspending our own Legislatures, and declaring themselves invested with power to legislate for us in all cases whatsoever.

He has abdicated Government here by declaring us out of his Protection and waging War against us.

He has plundered our seas, ravaged our Coasts, burnt our towns, and destroyed the lives of our people.

He is at this time transporting large Armies of foreign Mercenaries to complete the works of death, desolation and tyranny, already begun with circumstances of cruelty and perfidy scarcely paralleled in the most barbarous ages, and totally unworthy the Head of a civilized nation.

He has constrained our fellow Citizens taken Captive on the high Seas to bear Arms against their Country, to become the executioners of their friends and Brethren, or to fall themselves by their Hands.

He has excited domestic insurrections amongst us, and has endeavoured to bring on the inhabitants of our frontiers, the merciless Indian Savages, whose known rule of warfare is an undistinguished destruction of all ages, sexes and conditions.

In every stage of these Oppressions We have Petitioned for Redress in the most humble terms. Our repeated Petitions have been answered only by repeated injury. A Prince, whose character is thus marked by every act which may define a Tyrant, is unfit to be the ruler of a free people.

Nor have We been wanting in attentions to our British brethren.

We have warned them from time to time of attempts by their legislature to extend an unwarrantable jurisdiction over us.

We have reminded them of the circumstances of our emigration and settlement here.

We have appealed to their native justice and magnanimity, and we have conjured them by the ties of our common kindred to disavow these usurpations, which would inevitably interrupt our connections and correspondence.

They too have been deaf to the voice of justice and of consanguinity. We must, therefore, acquiesce in the necessity, which denounces our Separation, and hold them, as we hold the rest of mankind, Enemies in War, in Peace Friends.

We, therefore, the Representatives of the United States of America, in General Congress, Assembled, appealing to the Supreme Judge of the world for the rectitude of our intentions, do, in the Name, and by the authority of the good People of these Colonies, solemnly publish and declare.

That these United Colonies are, and of Right ought to be Free and Independent States; that they are Absolved from all Allegiance to the British Crown, and that all political connection between them and the State of Great Britain is and ought to be totally dissolved; and that as Free and Independent States, they have full Power to levy War, conclude Peace, contract Alliances, establish Commerce, and to do all other Acts and Things which Independent States may of right do. And for the support of this Declaration, with a firm reliance on the protection of Divine Providence, we mutually pledge to each other our Lives, our Fortunes, and our sacred Honor.

The signers of the Declaration represented the new States as follows:

New Hampshire:
Josiah Bartlett, William Whipple, Matthew Thornton

Massachusetts:
John Hancock, Samual Adams, John Adams, Robert Treat Paine, Elbridge Gerry

Rhode Island:
Stephen Hopkins, William Ellery

Connecticut:
Roger Sherman, Samuel Huntington, William Williams, Oliver Wolcott

New York:
William Floyd, Philip Livingston, Francis Lewis, Lewis Morris

New Jersey:
Richard Stockton, John Witherspoon, Francis Hopkinson, John Hart, Abraham Clark

Pennsylvania:
Robert Morris, Benjamin Rush, Benjamin Franklin, John Morton, George Clymer, James Smith, George Taylor, James Wilson, George Ross

Delaware:
Caesar Rodney, George Read, Thomas McKean

Maryland:
Samuel Chase, William Paca, Thomas Stone, Charles Carroll of Carrollton

Virginia:

George Wythe, Richard Henry Lee, Thomas Jefferson, Benjamin Harrison, Thomas Nelson, Jr., Francis Lightfoot Lee, Carter Braxton

North Carolina:

William Hooper, Joseph Hewes, John Penn

South Carolina:

Edward Rutledge, Thomas Heyward, Jr., Thomas Lynch, Jr., Arthur Middleton

Georgia:

Button Gwinnett, Lyman Hall, George Walton

Let this be our Declaration:

America — again,
One Nation Under God!

Let it be! So help us God.

So...Help us God!

Notes

Notes

Notes

Notes

Notes

Notes